Koha 3 Library Management System

Install, configure, and maintain your Koha installation with this easy-to-follow guide

Savitra Sirohi

Amit Gupta

[PACKT] open source ✳
PUBLISHING   community experience distilled

BIRMINGHAM - MUMBAI

Koha 3 Library Management System

First published: November 2010

Production Reference: 1091110

Published by Packt Publishing Ltd.
32 Lincoln Road
Olton
Birmingham, B27 6PA, UK.

ISBN 978-1-849510-82-0

www.packtpub.com

Cover Image by John M. Quick (john.m.quick@gmail.com)

Credits

Authors
Savitra Sirohi
Amit Gupta

Reviewers
Kyle M Hall
Vimal Kumar V

Acquisition Editor
Steven Wilding

Development Editor
Wilson D'souza

Technical Editor
Kavita Iyer

Indexer
Hemangini Bari

Editorial Team Leader
Akshara Aware

Project Team Leader
Priya Mukherji

Project Coordinator
Srimoyee Ghoshal

Proofreaders
Aaron Nash
Clyde Jenkins

Graphics
Nilesh Mohite

Production Coordinator
Adline Swetha Jesuthas

Cover Work
Adline Swetha Jesuthas

About the Authors

Savitra Sirohi heads Nucsoft OSS Labs (http://www.osslabs.biz) – a
Koha services provider. As part of his work, Savitra has lead several Koha
implementations and conducts regular Koha workshops in India. Savitra is an
Engineer and has an MBA from the Indian Institute of Management.

We would like to thank Kyle Hall, Vimal Kumar, and Nicole Engard
and other members of the Koha community who took the time to
review the chapter drafts. Their perspective and expertise helped
improve this book immeasurably.

Many thanks are due to Wilson, Kavita, Srimoyee, Steven, and others
at Packt for their expertise and hard work and also their patience
with these first time authors.

Amit Gupta is the lead Koha specialist at Nucsoft OSS Labs (http://www.
osslabs.biz), a Koha services provider. Amit has played a key role in several Koha
implementations, including the one at Delhi Public Library, one of India's biggest
Koha projects. Amit has a BSc and a Master's in Computer Applications.

About the Reviewers

Kyle M Hall is an IT specialist for the Meadville Public Library and the Crawford County Federated Library System of Pennsylvania is a Free Open Source Software advocate and software developer. His contributions to Koha include bugfixes and new features, as well as the Koha Off-line Circulation system. In addition to his work with Koha, he is also the author of a FOSS Kiosk Management System, Libk (`http://libki.org`), a cross-platform system for controlling access to computers via logins and time limits.

Vimal Kumar is a library professional with genuine interest in Linux and open source software. He is an active member of Koha community. He has a Master's degree in Library and Information Science from University of Kerala. He has done an evaluative study of open source library management system conducted in 2005 for the completion of MLISc degree project. During the past few years he has been active as a resource person for Koha training programs. He has been working with Mahatma Gandhi University Library and has also presented many papers in national and international conferences.

Table of Contents

Preface

Much of what we have written in this book is based on our experiences teaching Koha installation and maintenance of technology and library staff.

We hope this book will help you to quickly install and set up a working Koha installation, complete with catalog data migrated from your current library system. The first nine chapters of this book are devoted to these topics. In the rest of the book we cover topics such as troubleshooting, installing software updates, and customizing Koha, which will be of interest to you when you start to use Koha in earnest.

You will need some Linux expertise. Most Koha users use Debian. However you should feel free to try the installation on your preferred distribution. In the examples in this book, we have demonstrated Debian and openSuSE commands; we think these two are representative of most commonly used Linux distributions.

During the installation process, we would encourage you to seek help from the Koha community via the Koha mailing lists.

What this book covers

Chapter 1, Installing the Software Stack

In the first chapter our goal will be to install Koha's software stack — the Koha application itself, MySQL database server, Apache2 web server, and the various system and Perl packages Koha uses.

Chapter 2, Configuring the Apache2 Web Server

Next, we will configure Koha's web server — Apache2. Apache2 serves Koha pages to users when they access the OPAC or the staff client.

Chapter 3, Installing Koha's Zebra Search Engine

In the third chapter we will focus on Zebra—Koha's powerful catalog search engine. We will learn how to install and test Zebra.

Chapter 4, Koha's Web Installer, Crontab, and Other Server Configurations

In the fourth chapter, we will learn about executing Koha's web installer, setting up Koha's Crontab, and configuring Koha services to start automatically when the machine reboots. At the end of this chapter, we will be able to launch Koha.

Chapter 5, Configuring the Cataloging Module

This chapter is the first of three application configuration chapters. In this chapter, we will learn how to configure Koha's Cataloging module, which is used to maintain information about items in the library.

Chapter 6, Configuring the Circulation Module

In this chapter, we will learn how to configure Koha's circulation module. This module is used to loan library items to the patrons. Our goal here will be to map the library's circulation policies to rules and preferences in Koha.

Chapter 7, Configuring Other System Preferences

In this chapter, we will learn how to configure system preferences related to the rest of Koha's modules—Patrons, Acquisitions and Serials, and Online Public Access Catalog (OPAC). We will also study preferences related to styling and appearance, messaging, security, and search.

Chapter 8, Test Driving Your Koha Installation

By now we will be in a position to take our Koha installation for a test drive. We will look to complete a transaction cycle in each of the primary Koha modules—Patrons, Cataloging, Circulation, Acquisitions and Serials. We will also test the reports module and catalog search on the OPAC.

Chapter 9, Migrating Catalog Data

Migrating catalog data from the legacy system is a prerequisite to using Koha for most libraries. In this chapter we will learn how to convert MARC files from legacy systems into Koha compatible files. We will learn about Koha's MARC record import tools.

Chapter 10, Troubleshooting

In this chapter, we will learn about ways to troubleshoot Koha problems, we will learn about the community tools and resources and take a closer look at ten specific problems.

Chapter 11, Updating Software

It is good practice to keep your Koha software updated to benefit from new features and bug fixes, but also to avoid migration problems if your version falls too far behind. In this chapter we learn how to download and install software updates.

Chapter 12, Customizing Koha Software

Most serious Koha users will want to customize the software to suit their needs, perhaps to modify the styling or appearance or to tweak a certain page to show additional information. If you have the skills you can even take on more serious work such as adding new features. In this chapter, we learn how to customize Koha code.

Chapter 13, Advanced Topics

In this final chapter, we will learn about setting up some less widely used but nevertheless important features of Koha—custom record matching rules, LDAP authentication, custom OPACs for each library, internationalization, and setting up Koha as a Z39.50 source.

What you need for this book

You will need:

- A computer or a server
- A Linux DVD; we cover Debian & openSuSE in this book, but other distributions should be fine too
- High speed Internet connection to download software

Who this book is for

This book is aimed at Linux System Administrators who need to install and maintain Koha. If you are a system administrator who wants to set up an open source integrated library system, then this book is for you. It will also be useful for system administrators who require help with specific aspects of implementing Koha.

Conventions

In this book, you will find a number of styles of text that distinguish between different kinds of information. Here are some examples of these styles, and an explanation of their meaning.

Code words in text are shown as follows: "We use the `ln` command to create the symbolic link."

Any command-line input or output is written as follows:

```
koha@li190-245:/$ sudo ln -s /home/koha/koha-dev/etc/koha-httpd.conf /
etc/apache2/sites-available/koha-httpd.conf
```

New terms and **important words** are shown in bold. Words that you see on the screen, in menus or dialog boxes for example, appear in the text like this: "To edit these preferences, navigate to **Administration | Global system preferences.**".

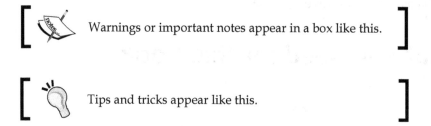

Warnings or important notes appear in a box like this.

Tips and tricks appear like this.

Reader feedback

Feedback from our readers is always welcome. Let us know what you think about this book—what you liked or may have disliked. Reader feedback is important for us to develop titles that you really get the most out of.

To send us general feedback, simply send an e-mail to feedback@packtpub.com, and mention the book title via the subject of your message.

If there is a book that you need and would like to see us publish, please send us a note in the **SUGGEST A TITLE** form on www.packtpub.com or e-mail suggest@packtpub.com.

If there is a topic that you have expertise in and you are interested in either writing or contributing to a book, see our author guide on www.packtpub.com/authors.

Customer support

Now that you are the proud owner of a Packt book, we have a number of things to help you to get the most from your purchase.

Errata

Although we have taken every care to ensure the accuracy of our content, mistakes do happen. If you find a mistake in one of our books—maybe a mistake in the text or the code—we would be grateful if you would report this to us. By doing so, you can save other readers from frustration and help us improve subsequent versions of this book. If you find any errata, please report them by visiting http://www.packtpub.com/support, selecting your book, clicking on the **errata submission form** link, and entering the details of your errata. Once your errata are verified, your submission will be accepted and the errata will be uploaded on our website, or added to any list of existing errata, under the Errata section of that title. Any existing errata can be viewed by selecting your title from http://www.packtpub.com/support.

Piracy

Piracy of copyright material on the Internet is an ongoing problem across all media. At Packt, we take the protection of our copyright and licenses very seriously. If you come across any illegal copies of our works, in any form, on the Internet, please provide us with the location address or website name immediately so that we can pursue a remedy.

Please contact us at copyright@packtpub.com with a link to the suspected pirated material.

We appreciate your help in protecting our authors, and our ability to bring you valuable content.

Questions

You can contact us at questions@packtpub.com if you are having a problem with any aspect of the book, and we will do our best to address it.

Installing the Software Stack 1

In this chapter, our goal will be to install Koha's software stack—the Koha application itself and the various system and Perl packages it uses. Installing the stack in itself is not enough to be able to use Koha, but is an important first step.

This task can be quite challenging, especially for novice Linux users. You will need to get familiar with using the Linux terminal and multiple installation tools. Expect problems with Perl modules, as troubleshooting these can be especially difficult.

We cover the chapter in three stages—first an orientation, next preparatory steps, and finally a demonstration of the installation. Throughout this book we will use two Linux distributions—Debian and openSuSE; the two combined are representative of most other distributions.

An orientation to Koha's installation

In this section we'll learn about:

- What components we will need to install
- What installation tools to use and when
- The implications of choosing one Linux distribution over another
- Where to get help when you run into installation problems

Koha's architecture

First, let us take a quick look at Koha's architecture. Koha runs on the Linux, Apache2, MySQL, Perl (LAMP) platform:

- **Linux**: The operating system
- **Apache2**: The web server
- **MySQL**: The database server
- **Perl**: Koha is written in the Perl programming language

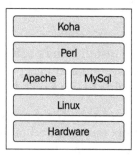

What do we need to install?

We will install various packages related to:

- The Koha architecture above—Linux, Apache, MySQL, and Perl
- The Koha application itself
- Build and compiler programs that help with the installation
- Various Perl and non Perl packages that Koha uses, along with their own prerequisites

Installation tools

Let us take a look at the various tools we will use to install Koha's software stack. These tools are:

- **Package manager**: To install Linux packages
- **Make utility**: To install Perl modules
- **CPAN shell**: To install Perl modules that are not available as Linux packages
- **Git**: To download the Koha application

Package manager

A package manager makes installation easy by automatically installing prerequisites, tracking versions and updates, and verifying checksums. Your choice of the package manager will usually depend on the Linux distribution you use. Here are some popular package managers:

- **APT**: On Debian or Ubuntu
- **YaST**: On openSuSE
- **YUM**: On CentOS

Make utility

Perl programs such as Koha or the various Perl modules it uses can be installed using a series of commands:

- `perl Makefile.PL`: This command checks for prerequisites and creates a configuration file needed by make
- `make`: This compiles the software and creates executables
- `make test`: It runs test cases to ensure proper installation, flags errors, and warnings in case of problems
- `make Install`: This installs the executable files into proper directories in the server

CPAN shell

CPAN (Comprehensive Perl Archive Network) — is an archive of Perl modules.

The CPAN shell is a tool that automates the download and installation of Perl modules from the archive including the execution of the `perl Makefile.PL`, `make`, `make test`, and `make` install commands given above.

Learn more about CPAN here: `http://www.cpan.org/`.

Git

Git is Koha's version control system. Git simplifies and automates the download of software from Koha's online repository. We use Git not only during installation, but also while installing software updates. If you wish to make software changes of your own, Git will help merge those changes with new versions of Koha.

Learn more about Git here: `http://git-scm.com/`.

Choosing between Linux Perl packages and CPAN modules

CPAN is the largest archive of Perl modules. Perl modules are always available on CPAN. Many, but not all of Koha's Perl prerequisites are available as packages in a distribution's sources.

The recommended approach in such a scenario is to use Linux packages where available. If you don't find packages for a certain module, then use CPAN to install it.

The Linux package manager can manage all prerequisites of a module. CPAN only knows about Perl prerequisites, and cannot install any non-Perl prerequisites. For this reason, you will likely have smoother installations with the package manager in comparison to CPAN.

Choosing a Linux distribution

It appears that Debian is the most popular when it comes to Koha. Some of the installation tasks are simpler in this distribution. Also you might get better community support from a large pool of Debian Koha users.

However, if you are skilled on another distribution, it might make sense to use that. Installation on Ubuntu is very similar to that on Debian. There are many Koha users on Fedora, CentOS, or openSuSE. Installation documents, live CDs, and other sorts of help are becoming available for these distributions as well.

In any case, once you are past the installation stage, it does not really matter distribution you are on.

Getting help—Koha's community resources

If you face trouble with the installation, Koha's community resources can be of excellent help:

- **Mailing lists**: Koha's mailing lists are very active and you are likely to get timely help. Join the mailing lists via this page: `http://koha-community.org/support/koha-mailing-lists/`.

- **Mailing lists archives**: Many of the discussions are indexed by search engines. If you run into trouble, it is likely someone else had a similar problem before you, so just search for solutions using your favourite search engine.

- **IRC chat**: Many of Koha's developers are available on this live chat forum. Join here: `http://koha-community.org/support/`.

- **Wiki**: Koha's wiki might have useful material - `http://wiki.koha-community.org/`.

- **Installation documents**: Up-to-date installation documents are available in Koha's application folder.

Preparing for installation

In this section we prepare for the installation—setting up a server, preparing a list of packages for installation and configuring installation tools.

Server prerequisites

Before we start the installation, we will need a server setup as follows:

Prerequisites	Description
Server	2 GB RAM, 40 GB hard disk should be good for most libraries.
Internet connection	High speed Internet connection to download software.
Linux	Your preferred distribution installed on the server.
Firewall ports opened	Git port 9418
	FTP port 21
	HTTP port 80
Access	Access to the server via SSH, or directly.
User	A Linux user with sudo privileges, in this book we use user—koha.
Locale	Your locale setup on the server.

Downloading Koha and switching to a branch

One of the first things we do is to download Koha and switch to a version (or a branch) that we want to use. This helps us draw up, as explained in sections below, our package installation list.

Cloning Koha

To download the Koha application, we need Git. Let us install Git:

```
koha@li190-245:~$ sudo apt-get install git
```

Now we are ready to download Koha, let us change to a folder where we want to install Koha. The user koha must own this folder:

```
koha@li190-245:~ # cd /home/koha
```

To **clone** the application from Koha's git server we use the `git clone` command:

```
koha@li190-245:~$ git clone git:://git.koha-community.org/koha.git
kohaclone
```

Checking out a branch

Before installing Koha, we need to select the software version or branch that we want to use. In production environments, you may want to use the stable version. In test environments you might want to use the latest version — master.

Let us say we want to install the stable version. A quick check on `http://git.koha-community.org` tells us that at the time of writing this chapter, the correct name of the stable branch is **v3.00.06.**

To use Git, we need to be in the `kohaclone` folder:

```
koha@ li190-245:/home/koha # cd kohaclone
```

To switch to this branch, we use the `git checkout` command:

```
koha@li190-245:~/kohaclone$ git checkout -b koha-stable v3.00.06
```

Preparing a list of installation packages

Preparing a list of installation packages can be a challenge depending on which distribution you are on. At the time of writing, package lists are available for Debian and Ubuntu only. We cannot use the same packages on other distributions — some packages may be named differently, and others may not be available at all. Also some packages that Koha requires may be available on your distribution and not on Debian and Ubuntu.

System packages

We use the term system packages for non-Perl modules. Here is a list of system packages that you must have in your installation list; you will need to to look up the right names for each of these from your distribution's sources:

Package	Description
Apache2	The web server.
MySQL	The database server.
Make	Programs that helps build and install packages.
Gcc	Is the compiler package.
Yaz	Is the toolkit used in Z39.50 clients and servers.
Libyaz	YAZ related libraries.
Libyaz-devel	YAZ related development libraries.

On Debian, to look up the name of a package we use the apt-cache search command:

```
koha@li190-245:~$ sudo apt-cache search libyaz
```

On openSuSE, we use the search tool available inside the YaST GUI:

```
koha@li190-245:~$ yast
```

Perl modules

An accurate list of Perl modules can be drawn up by running Koha's `Makefile.PL` program. The program checks for the installation status of Koha's Perl module prerequisites and displays warning messages for each missing module.

We run Koha's `Makefile.PL` program as follows:

```
koha@li190-245:~/kohaclone$ perl Makefile.PL
```

See the section on `Makefile.PL` below to see how to choose various options, or you can choose default value for now. The missing module prerequisites will be displayed at the end:

```
[Thu Aug  5 05:07:41 2010] Makefile.PL: Warning: prerequisite
PDF::Reuse::Barcode 0.05 not found.
[Thu Aug  5 05:07:41 2010] Makefile.PL: Warning: prerequisite
SMS::Send 0.05 not found.
[Thu Aug  5 05:07:41 2010] Makefile.PL: Warning: prerequisite
Schedule::At 1.06 not found.
[Thu Aug  5 05:07:41 2010] Makefile.PL: Warning: prerequisite
Text::CSV::Encoded 0.09 not found.
[Thu Aug  5 05:07:41 2010] Makefile.PL: Warning: prerequisite
```

```
Text::CSV_XS 0.32 not found.
[Thu Aug  5 05:07:41 2010] Makefile.PL: Warning: prerequisite XML::RSS
1.31 not found.
Writing Makefile for koha
koha@li190-245:~/kohaclone$
```

You will need to look up these modules in your distribution's repositories to find corresponding packages. The system packages will usually be named with a prefix "perl-" and will have "-" instead of "::". As an example, the Perl module PDF::Reuse::Barcode should have a corresponding Perl package called perl-PDF-Reuse-Barcode.

If you don't find some of the modules in your distribution's sources, then those modules will need to be installed using CPAN.

Debian/Ubuntu package lists

Package lists are available for Debian and Ubuntu in the kohaclone folder:

```
koha@li190-245:~/kohaclone$ vi install_misc/debian.packages
```

Or

```
koha@li190-245:~/kohaclone$ vi install_misc/ubuntu.packages
```

If you are on another distribution use the debian.packages or ubuntu.packages lists to look for corresponding modules in your distribution's sources.

It is important to note that these lists may not be completely accurate. This is because software changes all the time; for instance a package that was hitherto unavailable in Debian sources may become available when a new Debian version is released. So it might be a good idea to look for additional Perl packages in your Linux sources before installing them using CPAN.

Setting up repositories or sources

You might need to configure additional repositories or sources for some of the packages in your installation list.

With Debian you will need to add Index data's sources for YAZ related packages. Edit the sources file:

```
koha@li190-245:~$ sudo vi /etc/apt/sources.list
```

And add these lines to set up Index data's Debian package sources:

```
# Index Data
```

```
deb http://ftp.indexdata.dk/debian lenny main
deb-src http://ftp.indexdata.dk/debian lenny main
```

With openSuSE 11.2, you will need the Perl repository:

```
http://download.opensuse.org/repositories/devel:/languages:/perl/
openSUSE_11.2/
```

We use zypper to add a repository from the command line:

```
koha@li190-245:~$ sudo zypper ar http://download.opensuse.org/
repositories/devel:/languages:/perl/openSUSE_11.2/ perl-repository
```

Don't forget to refresh the package source. On Debian:

```
koha@li190-245:~$ sudo apt-get update
```

On openSuSE:

```
koha@li190-245:~$ sudo zypper refresh
```

Configuring the CPAN shell

We will need to configure the CPAN shell before we can use it to install Perl modules. To launch the shell we use the cpan command:

```
koha@linux:/home/koha/kohaclone # sudo cpan
```

You can choose to configure CPAN automatically:

```
Would you like me to configure as much as possible automatically? [yes]
yes
```

Or you can run through the steps manually.

Once the configuration completes, you should be in the CPAN shell:

```
commit: wrote '/usr/lib/perl5/5.10.0/CPAN/Config.pm'
Exiting subroutine via last at /usr/lib/perl5/5.10.0/CPAN.pm line 1450,
<STDIN> line 1.

cpan shell -- CPAN exploration and modules installation (v1.9205)
ReadLine support enabled

cpan[1] >
```

Installing Koha's software stack

In this final section we demonstrate the installation steps on Debian and openSUSE.

Installing packages using the package manager

We will install most packages using the package manager. Having installed Git in an earlier section, readers are already familiar with the commands used to install individual packages; in this section, we also look at ways of speeding up the process.

Installing packages from the Linux prompt

You can install the packages one-by-one like this:

```
koha@li190-245:~/kohaclone> sudo apt-get install apache2
```

On openSuSE, the command would look like this:

```
koha@li190-245:~/kohaclone> sudo yast -i apache2
```

Or you can install multiple packages in one statement:

```
koha@li190-245:~/kohaclone> sudo apt-get install apache2 mysql make gcc
```

Or:

```
koha@li190-245:~/kohaclone> sudo yast -i apache2 mysql make gcc
```

Installing packages using shell scripts

To speed up the installation, you can write a shell script file that looks like this:

```
yast -i apache2 \
mysql \
make \
gcc \
yaz \
libyaz \
libyaz-devel \
perl-Algorithm-CheckDigits \
perl-Biblio-EndnoteStyle \
```

And execute this script using the sh command:

```
koha@li190-245:~> sudo sh yast-opensuse-perl.sh
```

Installing packages using dselect

Debian and Ubuntu users can use `dselect`, a convenient way to install package lists.

First we install `dselect`:

```
koha@li190-245:~/kohaclone$ sudo apt-get install dselect
```

Next, we select what needs to be installed by pointing to the file containing the list of packages:

```
koha@li190-245:~/kohaclone$ sudo dpkg --set-selections < install_misc/
debian.packages
```

Finally we install the selected packages:

```
koha@li190-245:~/kohaclone$ sudo dselect
```

From the dselect screen, we will need to execute the install, configure, and delete options in sequence.

Installing Perl modules using CPAN

We use the CPAN shell to install only those Perl modules that are not available in your distribution's sources.

We can install such modules from inside the CPAN shell, like this:

```
koha@li190-245:~/kohaclone$ sudo cpan
cpan[1]> install HTTP::OAI
```

Install multiple modules using a single statement:

```
cpan[2]> install IPC::Cmd Net::LDAP Net::LDAP::Filter
Net::Z3950::ZOOM Text::CSV::Encoded
```

Another way of doing it is from the Linux shell:

```
koha@li190-245:~> sudo cpan HTTP::OAI
```

Here is how we install modules from the Linux shell:

```
koha@li190-245:~> sudo cpan IPC::Cmd Net::LDAP Net::LDAP::Filter
Net::Z3950::ZOOM Text::CSV::Encoded
```

Troubleshooting CPAN installations

If CPAN modules don't install successfully, we would see messages like these at the end of install command:

```
MIRK/Net-Z3950-ZOOM-1.26.tar.gz               : writemakefile NO
'/usr/bin/perl Makefile.PL INSTALLDIRS=site' returned status 512
 WRW/Barcode-Code128-2.01.tar.gz              : make_test NO
 LARSLUND/PDF-Reuse-Barcode-0.05.tar.gz       : make_test NO one
dependency not OK (Barcode::Code128)
cpan[8]>
```

From the messages above, we learn that the module Net-Z3950-ZOOM has failed at the Makefile.PL stage likely due to missing prerequisites.

The module PDF-Reuse-Barcode has failed to install, because one of its prerequisites—Barcode::Code128 has failed at the make test stage.

To troubleshoot such problems we need to look at error messages for clues. Resolve any problems that are found and then install each module manually using the make set of commands.

As an example, let us troubleshoot problems with installing the module Net-Z3950-ZOOM.

We use the look command to get into a Linux subshell:

```
cpan[8]> look Net::Z3950::ZOOM
Running look for module 'Net::Z3950::ZOOM'
Trying to open a subshell in the build directory...
Working directory is /home/koha/.cpan/build/Net-Z3950-ZOOM-1.26-C9NuSo
```

We run make clean to start afresh:

```
sh-3.2# make clean
make: *** No rule to make target 'clean'.  Stop.
```

Next run the Makefile.PL program:

```
sh-3.2# perl Makefile.PL
```

At this stage we see an error message indicating missing system packages:

```
ERROR: Unable to call script: yaz-config
If you are using a YAZ installation from the Debian package "yaz", you
will also need to install "libyaz-dev" in order to build this module.
```

This means we need to install YAZ related packages using the package manager, on Debian—yaz and libyaz-dev and on openSUSE—yaz, libyaz, libyaz-devel.

After installing these packages using the package manager, we run the make series of commands to complete the installation:

```
cpan[8]> look Net::Z3950::ZOOM
sh-3.2# make clean
sh-3.2# perl Makefile.PL
sh-3.2# make
sh-3.2# make test
sh-3.2# make install
sh-3.2# exit
cpan[8]>
```

Setting up Koha's MySQL database

Before we install Koha, we need to setup Koha's MySQL database and a MySQL user with privileges over the database.

Unless you have already done this as part of the installation, we first secure MySQL by configuring a password for the root users:

```
koha@li190-245:linux:/home/koha # mysqladmin -u root password
'yourdbrootpasswd';
```

Log in to MySQL using root:

```
koha@li190-245:~/kohaclone$ mysql -u root -p
Enter password:
```

Create Koha's database:

```
mysql> create database koha;
```

Create a MySQL user for Koha's database and grant it privileges. Both actions are accomplished with one command:

```
mysql> grant all on koha.* to 'kohaadmin'@'localhost' identified by
'katikoan';
mysql> flush privileges;
mysql> quit
```

Configuring Koha's installation: Makefile.PL

After we have installed required system and Perl packages and set up the database, we are ready to install Koha. The first step is to run `Makefile.PL` to configure Koha's installation. We will need to supply responses to questions such as mode of installation or database name:

```
koha@linux:/home/koha/kohaclone # perl Makefile.PL
```

Enter responses to configuration questions as follows:

Installation mode should be `dev` if you wish to use Git to apply patches.

```
Installation mode (dev, single, standard) [standard] dev
```

User koha must have write access to the configuration directory to avoid permissions problems:

```
Configuration directory: [/home/koha/koha-dev]
```

Choosing `mysql`, `Postgre` support in Koha is experimental:

```
DBMS to use (Pg, mysql) [mysql]
```

Here we specify the name of the database we created in an earlier step:

```
Please specify the name of the database to be used by Koha [koha]
```

Specify the MySQL user that has privileges over the database; we created this user in an earlier step:

```
Please specify the user that owns the database to be used by Koha
[kohaadmin]
```

Specify the password of this user:

```
Please specify the password of the user that owns the database to be used
by Koha [katikoan] katikoan
```

Say yes to Zebra – Koha's powerful catalog search engine; Although Koha can function without Zebra by using database indexes, Zebra's superior capabilities make it an important part of your installation:

```
Install the Zebra configuration files? (no, yes) [yes]
```

For other questions, the default value should be fine. Simply press the *Return* key to proceed to the next step.

The program display a summary of the configuration at the end, make a note of the details:

```
Koha will be installed with the following configuration parameters:
DB_HOST    localhost
DB_NAME    koha
DB_PASS    katikoan
DB_PORT    3306
DB_TYPE    mysql
DB_USER    kohaadmin
INSTALL_BASE    /home/koha/koha-dev
INSTALL_MODE dev
INSTALL_ZEBRA    yes
KOHA_INSTALLED_VERSION    3.01.00.124
RUN_DATABASE_TESTS    no
USE_MEMCACHED    no
```

If you have installed all prerequisites you should not see warning messages of missing prerequisites. If you do, you should go back and install any missing modules. Rerun `Makefile.PL` till all warnings disappear.

Completing Koha's installation

Run the following commands to complete the installation of Koha:

```
koha@li190-245:~/kohaclone$ make
koha@li190-245:~/kohaclone$ make test
koha@li190-245:~/kohaclone$ sudo make install
```

Summary

Here is what we learned in this chapter:

- Using Git to download and use a certain version of Koha
- Preparing an installation list for your distribution
- Installing packages using the package manager
- Installing Perl modules using the CPAN shell

- Troubleshooting Perl module installations
- Setting up Koha's MySQL database
- Installing Koha using the Make utility

In the next chapter, we will learn how to configure the Apache web server and Koha's web installer.

2
Configuring the Apache2 Web Server

In this chapter, our goal will be to configure Apache2. Apache2 is Koha's web server — it serves Koha pages to users when they access the OPAC (Online Public Access Catalog) or the staff client. At the end of the chapter we will be able to launch Koha's OPAC and the staff client interfaces using a web browser. However, the interfaces won't work until we execute Koha's web installer, a topic for *Chapter 4*.

We cover this chapter in three stages — first an orientation, next the preparatory steps, and finally a demonstration of the configuration. Again, we demonstrate the steps on two Linux distributions — Debian and openSuSE.

Understanding Apache2 configuration

In this section we try and understand what Apache2 is, how to configure different websites or applications that use it, and how the configuration differs across Linux distributions.

About Apache2

Apache is the world's most popular web server. It is used to serve static and dynamic pages to web browsers. Apache2 is a full featured web server. Koha uses it among other things for:

- Setting up two web interfaces, one for the OPAC and the other for the staff client
- Setting up of a host name for Koha, something like `http://koha.mylibrary.org/`

- Securing access to Koha's application folders
- Logging error messages to a file
- Rewriting page URLs

To learn more about Apache, refer to documentation here:

`http://httpd.apache.org/docs/2.2/`.

Apache2 virtual hosts

Apache's documentation (`http://httpd.apache.org/docs/2.2/vhosts/`) defines virtual hosts as follows:

> *The term Virtual Host refers to the practice of running more than one web site (such as* `www.company1.com` *and* `www.company2.com`*) on a single machine. Virtual hosts can be "IP-based", meaning that you have a different IP address for every web site, or "name-based", meaning that you have multiple names running on each IP address. The fact that they are running on the same physical server is not apparent to the end user.*

We will have two Koha virtual hosts—one for the OPAC and the other for its staff client.

Name-based or IP-based virtual hosts

Koha has two interfaces, the OPAC and the staff client. You will need to choose how you want to access these interfaces:

- With the same host name, but different port, say: `http://koha.mylibrary.org`, `http://koha.mylibrary.org:8080/`
- With two host names, say: `http://koha-opac.mylibrary.org` and `http://koha-staff.mylibrary.org`
- With an IP address and different ports, say: `http://192.168.1.21` and `http://192.168.1.21:8080`
- With two IP addresses, say: `http://192.168.1.21` and `http://192.168.1.22`

Here are some guidelines to help you work this out:

- Using host names is a better option because they are easier to remember. But if you are not in a position to create host names, you will need to use IP addresses.

- Using Apache2's default port 80 for both interfaces is a better choice. Port 80 is allowed for use on most networks.

- If you are not in a position to create two host names, you can consider using an additional port. Port 8080 is a popular alternative to port 80 and is allowed for use on many networks.

- If you are not in a position to use a second port for the staff client due to network or firewall constraints, you will need to use either two host names or two IP addresses.

- To use two IP addresses you will need a machine with two Network Interface Cards (NICs).

Apache2's configuration folder

The Apache2 web server can be configured by editing various files in its configuration folder. On many distributions this folder is named apache2 and is available under the /etc folder.

On other distributions it is named httpd.

It might be useful to browse this folder and get a sense of its contents:

```
koha@li190-245:/$ ls /etc/apache2/
```

Or use this command:

```
koha@li190-245:/$ ls /etc/httpd/
```

There are differences in how the Apache2 folder is organized in various distributions. For instance, on Debian Apache2 ports are configured in the ports.conf file. Let us take a brief look at this file:

```
koha@li190-245:/$ sudo vi /etc/apache2/ports.conf
```

On openSuSE however, this file is called listen.conf.

```
koha@li190-245:/$ sudo vi /etc/apache2/listen.conf
```

On Debian, virtual host files—essentially configuration files for each website or application that runs on the server—are set up in the folder sites-available:

```
koha@li190-245:/$ ls /etc/apache2/sites-available/
```

While on openSuSE such files are created in the folder `vhosts.d`:

```
koha@li190-245:/$ ls /etc/apache2/vhosts.d/
```

Koha's default Apache2 file

Koha's installation process from the previous chapter creates a default Apache2 configuration file named `koha-httpd.conf`.

You will find this file under the `etc` folder inside Koha's configuration folder. Take a look at this file:

```
koha@li190-245:/$ vi /home/koha/koha-dev/etc/koha-httpd.conf
```

Koha's virtual hosts

The file has two Apache2 virtual host blocks—one for Koha's OPAC and the other for its staff client.

This is what the OPAC virtual host looks like:

```
## OPAC
<VirtualHost 127.0.0.2:80>
  ServerAdmin webmaster@linux
  DocumentRoot /home/koha/kohaclone/koha-tmpl
...

...

</VirtualHost>
```

And the staff client virtual host is right below the OPAC block:

```
## Intranet
<VirtualHost 127.0.0.2:8080>
ServerAdmin webmaster@linux
DocumentRoot /home/koha/kohaclone/koha-tmpl

...

...

</VirtualHost>
```

Virtual host configuration

Each virtual host block has a set of directives that controls how Apache2 will work with respect to Koha.

You will find that the default `koha-httpd.conf` file is already configured for the most part, but we may want to modify some of the settings to suit our environment.

Some of the directives we may want to configure are:

Directive	Description
ServerAdmin	The e-mail address that is displayed when the website does not function properly.
ServerName	This is Koha's host name—something like `koha.mylibrary.org`.
ServerAlias	Any other domain that users may use, for example, `libcat.mylibrary.org`.
ErrorLog	The file to which Apache2 will write Koha related errors.
Directory	This directive controls what permissions Apache2 has on some of Koha's folders.

Preparing for Apache2 configuration

Now that we learned a bit about how to configure Apache2, here are some preparatory steps leading up to the configuration task. First we define a configuration plan; we also look at a list of configuration prerequisites.

Configuration plan

Here we define host names or IP addresses, ports, and other Apache2 directives for the OPAC and staff client virtual hosts. Here are some sample plans to help you develop your own.

Two host names

This is the best way to configure the two interfaces—there are two different host names, both easy to remember and we don't use any non-standard ports.

Item	Value	Comments
OPAC IP Address	Any	We use host based virtual hosts; we don't need to use IP based virtual hosts.
Staff Client IP Address	Any	Same as explained in OPAC IP Address.
OPAC Host Name	libcat.mylibrary.org	
Staff Client Host Name	libstaff.mylibrary.org	
OPAC Port	80	We have the ability to create host names; we don't need to use non-standard ports.
Staff Client Port	80	Same as explained in OPAC Port.
OPAC Error Log	/var/log/apache2/log/ koha-opac-error_log	We prefer to have all Apache2 logs under /var/ log/apache2.
Staff Client Error Log	/var/log/apache2/log/ koha-staff-error_log	Same as explained in OPAC Error Log.
Administrator Email Address	webmaster@mylibrary. org	

Hostname with two ports

Here we use a single host name but two different ports. As the staff client is usually used within the library, it is best to have that on a non-standard port, while the OPAC remains on port 80.

Item	Value	Comments
OPAC IP Address	Any	We use host based virtual hosts, we don't need to use IP addresses to identify different interfaces.
Staff Client IP Address	Any	Same as explained in OPAC IP Address.
OPAC Host Name	library.mylibrary.org	
Staff Client Host Name	library.mylibrary.org	

Item	Value	Comments
OPAC Port	80	
Staff Client Port	8080	We expect to use the staff client within our network, and using a non-standard port is not a problem for us.

IP address with two ports

If you are not in a position to setup hostnames, you would need to use IP addresses. Here we use a single IP address with two different ports.

Item	Value	Comments
OPAC IP Address	192.168.1.21	This is just a test environment; at this time we can't get a host name and a DNS entry.
Staff Client IP Address	192.168.1.21	Same as explained in OPAC IP Address.
OPAC Host Name	N/A	
Staff Client Host Name	N/A	
OPAC Port	80	
Staff Client Port	8080	We expect to use the staff client within our network, and using a non-standard port is not a problem for us.

Two IP addresses

This is IP based virtual hosts. We use two IP addresses, one for the OPAC and the other for the staff client. Your Koha server needs to have at least two Network Interfaces cards.

Item	Value	Comments
OPAC IP Address	192.168.1.21	This is just a test environment; here we can't get a host name and a DNS entry.
Staff Client IP Address	192.168.1.22	Our server has or we can setup two IP addresses.
OPAC Host Name	N/A	
Staff Client Host Name	N/A	
OPAC Port	80	
Staff Client Port	80	In our organization, it is difficult getting firewalls opened for non-standard port 8080.

Standalone machine

If you intend to use Koha on a standalone machine, then the plan is fairly straight forward. We use the machine's localhost address or the corresponding local loop IP address — 127.0.0.1. As the machine is not networked, it is easy to use port 8080 or any other port for that matter.

Item	Value	Comments
OPAC IP Address	127.0.0.1	We intend to use Koha on a standalone computer, so we use the local loop IP address.
Staff Client IP Address	127.0.0.1	Same as above.
OPAC Host Name	localhost	
Staff Client Host Name	localhost	
OPAC Port	80	
Staff Client Port	8080	Standalone computer; there are no problems using a non-standard port.

Configuration prerequisites

Here is a list of prerequisites that you might want to take care of; some of these may not apply to your situation depending on the sort of configuration plan you have.

Item	Description
Open Firewall ports	If you are using ports other port 80, you might need to open those ports on network firewalls or routers.
Host Names	If you intend to use host names, you will have to purchase or set them up.
Domain Name Service (DNS)	If you use host names, you will have to set them up in a DNS to route requests to the Koha server.
IP Addresses	If you are using IP based virtual hosts, you will need to ensure network cards are installed on your server.

Configuring Apache2 web server

Now that we have our configuration plan in place, let us get started with Apache2 configuration. We will edit the OPAC and staff client virtual hosts in Koha's Apache2 configuration file. We will also configure Apache2 to listen on the staff client port – 8080 and we will enable its Rewrite module. To make all this work we will point Apache2 to Koha's Apache2 configuration file using a symbolic link.

Creating a symbolic link to koha-httpd.conf

1. First we create a symbolic link in Apache2's virtual host's folder pointing to Koha's Apache2 file. A symbolic link is just a pointer to the actual Koha file.

2. We can copy the `koha-httpd.conf` file into the virtual host's folder, but it is better to create a symbolic link as this helps when new versions of the file are created during software upgrades.

3. We use the `ln` command to create the symbolic link. The syntax is:

   ```
   ln -s <path to koha-httpd.conf> <path to symbolink link name>
   ```

4. On Debian the command would be:

   ```
   koha@li190-245:/$ sudo ln -s /home/koha/koha-dev/etc/koha-httpd.
   conf /etc/apache2/sites-available/koha-httpd.conf
   ```

5. And on openSuSE, the command would look like this:

   ```
   koha@li190-245:/$ sudo ln -s /home/koha/koha-dev/etc/koha-httpd.
   conf /etc/apache2/vhosts.d/koha-httpd.conf
   ```

Enabling Apache2's Rewrite module

Koha uses Apache2's Rewrite module to manipulate URLs. To allow this we need to enable the module using the `a2enmod` command:

```
koha@li190-245:/$ sudo a2enmod rewrite
```

Configuring the listener

If you intend to use ports other than 80, you will need to configure the `Listen` directive. On Debian we add this directive to the `ports.conf` file:

```
koha@li190-245:/$ sudo vi /etc/apache2/ports.conf
```

And on openSuSE, we add this to the file `listen.conf`:

```
koha@li190-245:/$ sudo vi /etc/apache2/listen.conf
```

We add the directive in this manner:

```
Listen 8080
```

Editing the OPAC virtual host

Now we modify Koha's virtual hosts file to include elements of our configuration plan. First we set the IP address in the first line of the Virtual Host block. Something like this:

```
## OPAC
<VirtualHost 192.168.1.21:80>
```

If you want to use any IP address on the server, use "*":

```
## OPAC
<VirtualHost *:80>
```

Next we setup Koha's host name in the `ServerName` directive.

```
ServerName libcat.mylibrary.org
```

If are not using a host name, leave this Directive untouched.

Next, we add the `Directory` directive. Make sure you add these lines just before the `</virtualhost>` tag. Note that this step is not required on Debian.

```
    <Directory /home/koha/kohaclone>
        Order allow, deny
        Allow from all
    </Directory>
```

In a similar manner, we set other directives:

```
ServerAdmin  webmaster@mylibrary.org

ErrorLog  /var/log/apache2/log/koha-opac-error_log
```

Editing the staff client virtual host

Next we edit the staff client virtual host block; we will need to repeat the steps above for this virtual host.

If you need to change the port we edit the first line of the virtual host:

```
## Intranet
<VirtualHost 127.0.0.2:8080>
```

If the port needs to be port 80, we change the line as follows:

```
## Intranet
<VirtualHost 127.0.0.2:80>
```

Enabling Koha's virtual hosts

On some distributions we need to enable the new virtual host file. For instance on Debian, we run the a2ensite command to do this:

```
koha@li190-245:/etc/apache2/sites-available$ sudo a2ensite koha-httpd.
conf
```

```
Enabling site koha-http.conf.
```

The a2ensite command creates a symbolic link in the sites-enabled folder pointing to the Apache2 configuration file in the sites-available folder.

This step is not required openSuSE.

Restarting Apache2

Finally we restart Apache2 to load the new configuration changes:

```
linux:/etc/apache2/vhosts.d # sudo /etc/init.d/apache2 restart
Syntax OK
Shutting down httpd2 (waiting for all children to terminate)
                                              done
Starting httpd2 (prefork)
                                              done
Launching Koha
```

Once we complete the Apache2 configuration, we are ready to test Koha. To navigate to the OPAC, type the URL for the OPAC in your favorite browser.

Depending on your configuration, you may access the site via the host name, something like this:

```
http://libcat.mylibrary.org
```

Or using an IP address, like this:

```
http://192.168.1.21
```

If you are on a standalone machine, you would use a local loop IP address or the name localhost:

```
http://localhost or http://127.0.01
```

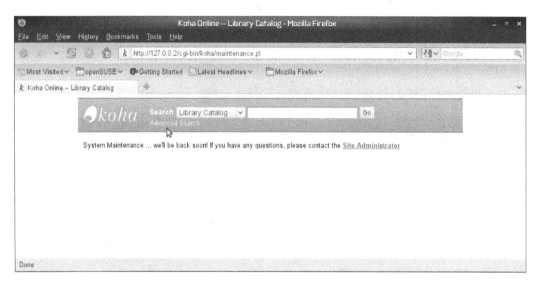

On the OPAC you will see a **System Maintenance** message; this is because we have not configured Koha's web installer yet.

To navigate to the staff client, type the URL for Koha's staff client:

```
http://libstaff.mylibrary.org/
```

Or if you are using a port 8080, something like this: `http://library.mylibrary.org:8080/`

Or if you are using an IP address with port 8080:

```
http://192.168.1.21:8080/
```

Or if have a dedicated IP address:

```
http://192.168.1.22/
```

Or if you are on a standalone machine:

```
http://localhost:8080 or http://127.0.0.1:8080/
```

This screen means we have successfully configured Apache2. In the next chapter, we will look at how to execute this web installer.

Troubleshooting configuration problems

Here is an explanation of some common problems with Apache2 configuration.

Rewrite module not enabled

If you have not enabled Apache2's Rewrite module, you will see this error when starting Apache2:

```
linux:/etc/apache2/vhosts.d # sudo /etc/init.d/apache2 restart
Syntax error on line 28 of /etc/apache2/vhosts.d/koha-httpd.conf:

    Invalid command 'RewriteEngine', perhaps misspelled or defined by a
    module not included in the server configuration
```

Incorrect or missing Directory directive

On distributions such as openSuSE, if you have not added the Directory directive, you will see this error when you try to access Koha's OPAC or the staff client. This means Apache2 does not have permission to access Koha's folders.

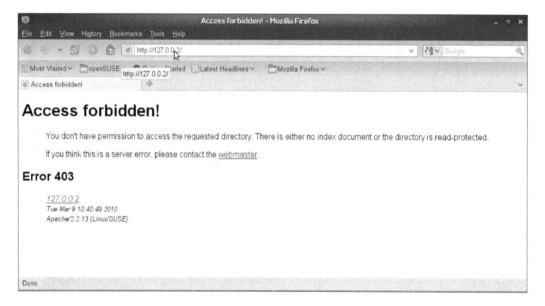

Unable to connect to MySQL

If the MySQL server is down or you dont have the Koha database set up properly, Koha and Apache2 will not be able to connect to the database and you will see this type of error:

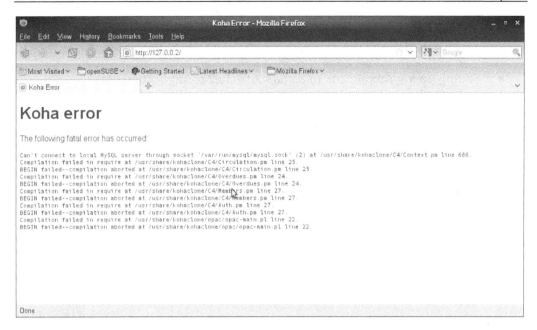

Listener not setup

If you do not setup the Apache2 listener for the staff client port, you will see this
error when you try to connect to Koha's staff client:

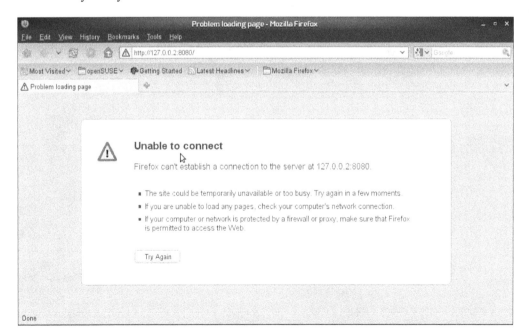

Summary

Here is what we learned in this chapter on configuring Apache2:

- Setting up a symbolic link to Koha's Apache2 configuration file
- Enabling Apache2's Rewrite module
- Configuring an IP address in Koha's virtual hosts
- Configuring host names in Koha's virtual hosts
- Setting up Apache2 to listen on the staff client port
- Configuring the Directory directive in a virtual host
- Launching Koha's OPAC and staff client

In the next chapter, we will install and test Koha's Zebra search engine.

3
Installing Koha's Zebra Search Engine

You will need to use Koha's Zebra search engine if you have more than say 10,000 catalog records. Without Zebra, catalog search results may be too slow.

If you have a small catalog you can use Koha without Zebra, in fact earlier versions of Koha did not have Zebra. Without Zebra both installation and ongoing maintenance will be simpler. However you should consider using Zebra even for small catalog sizes because of Zebra's superior capabilities.

In this chapter we will learn more about Zebra and how to install and test it.

About Zebra

From the website of Indexdata, the organization behind Zebra:

> "Zebra is a high-performance, general-purpose structured text indexing and retrieval engine. It reads structured records in a variety of input formats (eg. email, XML, MARC) and allows access to them through exact boolean search expressions and relevance-ranked free-text queries."

In our experience with Koha, we find Zebra to be an excellent search engine:

- It is fast and efficient
- It can index large databases
- It can index bibliographic, authority, and holdings records
- It is Unicode compliant and can work with any language
- It is highly configurable; you can index any MARC field, set up numeric, word, or phrase indexes, or configure ranking and sorting

- It can be queried using complex search expressions such as AND and OR operators

- It allows for additional features on Koha such as search limits, and refining searches that are otherwise not available

- It has sophisticated features such as approximate matching, and spelling correction

- It can be queried by any Z39.50 or SRU/W client

Learn more about Zebra here:

`http://www.indexdata.com/zebra/.`

Documentation on Zebra is available here:

`http://www.indexdata.com/zebra/doc/.`

Koha's Zebra related components

Before we install and test Zebra with Koha, let us understand a couple of key Zebra related components that we will use frequently as Koha administrators.

Zebrasrv—the Zebra query and retrieval server

This is a Zebra component that is responsible for serving results to search requests coming from Koha's OPAC or staff client. Here are some key points to note about `zebrasrv`:

- For search to function, the `zebrasrv` process must be running on the Koha server

- The process can be started by using the `zebrasrv` command from the Linux shell

- `zebrasrv` is usually run in the background as a service or a daemon

- To make `zebrasrv` work with our Koha installation, we will need to invoke the process by pointing it to use Koha's configuration file

Rebuild_zebra.pl—the Zebra index maintenance program

This is a Perl program that is used to create and maintain Zebra's search indexes. Here are some key points about this program:

- This is a Koha program that uses Zebra's `zebraidx` index maintenance utility
- The program can be used to build indexes in full or in an incremental fashion
- The program can be run form the Linux shell
- For ongoing index maintenance the program is usually scheduled to run in the Crontab

Installing Zebra

To get Koha working with Zebra we will need to install Zebra packages and then install Koha. You can skip this section if you have already installed Zebra, and have installed Koha by selecting the Zebra option during the `Makefile.PL` step.

Installing Zebra packages

 You might have already installed Zebra packages. These packages are part of the Debian and Ubuntu packages lists that we covered in *Chapter 1*. If you have indeed installed Zebra, you can skip this section.

On Debian we would install Zebra packages as follows:

```
koha@li190-245:~/kohaclone> sudo apt-get install idzebra-2.0-common
idzebra-2.0-doc idzebra-2.0 idezebra-2.0-utils
```

On openSuSE, the package names are different, so the installation command would look like this:

```
koha@li190-245:~/kohaclone> sudo yast -i idzebra idzebra-doc idzebra-
devel idzebra-debuginfo
```

Installing Koha with Zebra

 You might have already installed Koha with Zebra. If you had installed Zebra packages before installing Koha and had selected **yes** to the question **Install the Zebra configuration files?**, then you can skip this section.

Once Zebra packages are installed we need to install Koha. This installation process creates Zebra related configuration files and installs them in Koha's configuration folder, in our case /etc/koha-dev/.

To install Koha with Zebra, we run Koha Makefile.PL program:

```
koha@linux:/home/koha/kohaclone # perl Makefile.PL
```

Say yes to this question on installing Zebra configuration files:

```
Install the Zebra configuration files? (no, yes) [yes]
```

We then run the other make commands complete the installation of Koha with Zebra:

```
koha@li190-245:~/kohaclone$ make
koha@li190-245:~/kohaclone$ make test
koha@li190-245:~/kohaclone$ sudo make install
```

If you have had to reinstall Koha, you may need to reconfigure Apache2 (see *Chapter 2*) as the Koha installation process may have overwritten the Apache2 configuration file you created.

Testing Zebra

Now that we have installed Zebra, let us try out the zebrasrv command and the rebuild_zebra.pl program.

We will learn how to execute the zebrasrv command from the Linux shell and as a daemon. On production systems zebrasrv is usually run as a daemon that runs silently in the background.

The rebuild_zebra.pl command can also be executed from the Linux shell. On production systems however the program is scheduled to run in the crontab.

Testing zebrasrv

The `zebrasrv` program is usually installed under `/usr/bin` and you should be able to invoke it from any folder location.

The zebrasrv command

To learn more about how `zebrasrv` is used, we run the command with the `-help` or `-h` option:

```
linux-4yut:/home/koha # sudo zebrasrv --help
Usage: zebrasrv [ -a <pdufile> -v <loglevel> -l <logfile> -u <user> -c
<config> -t <minutes> -k <kilobytes> -d <daemon> -p <pidfile> -C
certfile -ziDST1 -m <time-format> -w <directory> <listener-addr>... ]
```

To learn more about each option, use the `man` command:

```
linux-4yut:/home/koha # man zebrasrv
```

Invoking zebrasrv with Koha's configuration file

To make `zebrasrv` use Koha's configuration file we use the `-f` option:

```
linux-4yut:/home/koha # sudo zebrasrv -f /etc/koha-dev/etc/koha-conf.xml
```

The process starts in the shell foreground and waits for search queries to serve:

```
...
14:25:24-22/04 [log] Loaded filter module
/usr/lib/idzebra-2.0/modules/mod-text.so
14:25:24-22/04 [server] Adding dynamic listener on
unix:/etc/koha-dev/var/run/zebradb/bibliosocket id=1
14:25:24-22/04 [server] Adding dynamic listener on
unix:/etc/koha-dev/var/run/zebradb/authoritysocket id=2
14:25:24-22/04 [server] Starting server zebrasrv pid=11088
```

To stop the server and to exit to the Linux shell, use *Ctrl+C* to:

```
^C
linux-4yut:/home/koha #
```

zebrasrv daemon

The Zebra Server is usually run in the background as a daemon. In this section we learn how to setup `zebrasrv` as a daemon and how to set it up as a service that can be included in the system's start-up profile. Once again, we see how things are easier on Debian or Ubuntu than on openSuSE.

Zebrasrv daemon on Debian or Ubuntu

Koha ships with a script, `koha-zebra-ctl.sh` that can run `zebrasrv` in the background as a daemon. This script uses the `daemon` command to start, stop, or restart Zebra.

You will need to ensure that the *daemon* package is installed:

```
linux-4yut:/home/koha # sudo apt-get install daemon
```

The script `koha-zebra-ctl.sh` can be found under the `bin` folder under Koha's configuration folder:

```
linux-4yut:/home/koha # cd /etc/koha-dev/bin/
linux-4yut:/etc/koha-dev/bin # vi koha-zebra-ctl.sh
```

Koha's Zebra daemon script can be set up as a service and configured in the system start-up profile. This way we ensure that `zebrasrv` starts automatically when the machine reboots. To set up the script as a service we create a symbolic link to it from the `/etc/init.d/` folder:

```
linux-4yut:/home/koha # sudo ln -s /etc/koha-dev/bin/koha-zebra-ctl.sh /
etc/init.d/koha-zebra-daemon
```

Let us test this `zebrasrv` service by starting it:

```
linux-4yut:/home/koha # sudo /etc/init.d/koha-zebra-daemon start
Starting Zebra Server
```

Let us try a `restart`:

```
linux-4yut:/home/koha # sudo /etc/init.d/koha-zebra-daemon restart
Restarting the Zebra Server
```

And finally let us try a `stop` operation:

```
linux-4yut:/home/koha # sudo /etc/init.d/koha-zebra-daemon stop
Stopping Zebra Server
```

To setup this service in the start-up profile, we use the `update-rc.d` command:

```
linux-4yut:/home/koha # sudo update-rc.d koha-zebra-daemon defaults
```

zebrasrv daemon on openSuSE

The daemon command is not available on openSuSE. This is because the corresponding package daemon is not included in openSuSE repositories for copyright reasons.

However there are alternatives to the daemon command:

- startproc: For starting a process
- killproc: For stopping a process

We can modify the koha-zebra-ctl.sh file to work on openSuSE by replacing the daemon command with startproc and killproc and suitably modifying the options supplied to the commands.

The modified statements in koha-zebra-ctl.sh script may look like this:

```
start)
echo "Starting Zebra Server"

startproc -l $ERRLOG $ZEBRASRV -f $KOHA_CONF


stop)
echo "Stopping Zebra Server"

killproc -TERM $ZEBRASRV


restart)
echo "Restarting the Zebra Server"

killproc -TERM $ZEBRASRV
startproc -l $ERRLOG $ZEBRASRV -f $KOHA_CONF
```

> You will need to reinstall Koha once you have modified the script to ensure that the modified koha-zebra-ctl.sh file is installed in Koha's configuration folder—/etc/koha-dev/bin/.

Once the script is modified and installed, we can set it up as a service by creating a symbolic link to it from the /etc/init.d folder:

```
linux-4yut:/home/koha # sudo ln -s /etc/koha-dev/bin/koha-zebra-ctl.sh /
etc/init.d/koha-zebra-daemon
```

To ensure that `zebrasrv` starts when the machine reboots we use the `chkconfig` command:

```
linux-4yut:/home/koha # sudo chkconfig koha-zebra-daemon on
```

Rebuilding Zebra

Let us now test the second key Zebra related component – `rebuild_zebra.pl`. This program is used to maintain Zebra's search indexes.

The program can be found in the folder `misc/migration_tools` under the `kohaclone` folder:

```
linux-4yut:/usr/share/kohaclone # cd misc/migration_tools/
linux-4yut:/usr/share/kohaclone/misc/migration_tools/ # vi rebuild_zebra.
pl
```

To learn about the usage of this program, run it with the `--help` or `--h` option:

```
linux-4yut:/home/koha # sudo ./rebuild_zebra.pl --help
./rebuild_zebra.pl: reindex MARC bibs and/or authorities in Zebra.
```

Use this batch job to reindex all biblio or authority records in your Koha database. This job is useful only if you are using Zebra; if you are using the 'NoZebra' mode, this job should not be used.

Parameters	Description
-b	Index bibliographic records.
-a	Index authority records.
-z	Select only updated and deleted records marked in the `zebraqueue` table. Cannot be used with -r or -s.
-r	Clear Zebra index before adding records to index.
-d	Temporary directory for indexing. If not specified, one is automatically created. The export directory is automatically deleted unless you supply the -k switch.
-k	Do not delete export directory.
-s	Skip export. Used if you have already exported the records in a previous run.
-noxml	Index from ISO MARC blob instead of MARC XML. This option is recommended only for advanced user.
-x	Export and index as XML instead of iso2709 (biblios only).Use this if you might have records > 99,999 chars.

Parameters	Description
-nosanitize	Export biblio/authority records directly from DB marcxml field without sanitizing records. It speed up dump process but could fail if DB contains badly encoded records. Works only with -x.
-w	Skip shadow indexing for this batch.
-y	Does NOT clear zebraqueue after indexing; normally, after doing batch indexing, zebraqueue should be marked done for the affected record type(s) so that a running zebraqueue_daemon doesn't try to reindex the same records—specify -y to override this. Cannot be used with -z.
-v	Increase the amount of logging. Normally only warnings and errors from the indexing are shown.
-munge-config	Deprecated option to try to fix Zebra config files.
--help or -h	Show this message.

Here are some key points about the options available with the rebuild_zebra.pl program:

- The most commonly used options are -b, -a, -r, -z, -v, and -x.
- We use either -r or -z, not both.
- Both -b and -a can be used in the same statement.
- If we expect at least some MARC records to have large sizes we use -x, for instance if the number of holdings is very large.
- The -v option can be used to troubleshoot problems with the program.
- The -r option is typically used when the server is setup and catalog data has been migrated.
- The -r option should also be used if Zebra configuration is changed, for instance if a new field is to be indexed.
- The -z option should be used when the rebuild program is scheduled in the crontab. This option only indexes updates to the catalog.

Let us look at some examples to learn how to run this program.

Creating or recreating indexes

To create or recreate the complete index of all bibliographic records in the database, we would run the command as follows:

```
linux-4yut:/usr/share/kohaclone/misc/migration_tools # sudo ./rebuild_
zebra.pl -b -r -v
```

To index bibliographic records incrementally, we could set up the command as follows:

```
linux-4yut:/usr/share/kohaclone/misc/migration_tools # sudo ./rebuild_
zebra.pl -b -z -v
```

To index both bibliographic and authority records incrementally, we would set up the command as follows:

```
linux-4yut:/usr/share/kohaclone/misc/migration_tools # sudo ./rebuild_
zebra.pl -b -a -z -v
```

If you have at least some records of large sizes, it is recommended that we use the –x option:

```
linux-4yut:/usr/share/kohaclone/misc/migration_tools # sudo ./rebuild_
zebra.pl -b -a -z -x -v
```

Using Koha without Zebra

If you decide that you do not want to use Zebra, you will need to ensure that the system preference **NoZebra** is turned on. We will learn about Koha's system preferences in subsequent chapters.

If you have installed Koha with Zebra and you want to stop using it, you will need to run a Koha program `rebuild_nozebra.pl`. This needs to be run just once when you start to use Koha without Zebra. The command is executed as follows:

```
linux-4yut:/usr/share/kohaclone/misc/migration_tools # ./rebuild_nozebra.
pl
```

Summary

Here is what we learned in this chapter:

- Installing Zebra packages
- Installing or reinstalling Koha to work with Zebra
- Invoking the `zebrasrv` program from the Linux shell
- Running the `zebrasrv` as a daemon
- Setting up the `zebrasrv` daemon as a service
- Including the `zebrasrv` service in the start-up profile
- Executing the `rebuild_zebra.pl` program with different options
- Turning off Zebra

In the next chapter, we will complete the installation process by executing Koha's web installer and configuring the Crontab to schedule Zebra and other programs.

4
Koha's Web Installer, Crontab, and Other Server Configurations

In this chapter, we will complete Koha's installation and system configuration tasks. First we will execute Koha's web installer to populate the Koha database structure and some important administrative settings. This will allow us to launch Koha's staff interface and its OPAC.

We will set up the koha user's crontab to schedule periodic execution of Koha programs such as those that generate overdue notices or calculate fines.

We will also set up an XML parser suitable for use with Koha.

Finally we will make sure Koha related services start automatically when the machine reboots.

Executing Koha's web installer

In this section of the chapter, we will learn how to execute Koha's web installer. The web installer performs several important functions such as creating Koha's database structure or populating mandatory administrative settings. It can also populate optional settings and sample data such as MARC frameworks or patron categories. The installer is launched from the staff client interface using Koha's MySQL user and is a series of interactive steps. At the end of the process we will be able to launch Koha's staff interface and its OPAC.

Understanding the web installer's functions

Koha's web installer performs the following functions:

- Checks for the existence of Koha's database, the connectivity to the database, and if the database user has the required privilege on the Koha database

- Creates Koha's database structure — its tables, relationships between tables, database constraints, and other rules

- Accepts user input on important configuration questions such as Language or MARC flavor

- Populates the Koha database with several mandatory administrative settings such as the default system preferences

- Populates the Koha database with several optional administrative settings and sample data such as MARC bibliographic frameworks, sample libraries, or sample patron categories

- Configures Koha catalog search to use Zebra or to use database indexing

Understanding how to execute the web installer

Here are some important points to note about executing Koha's web installer:

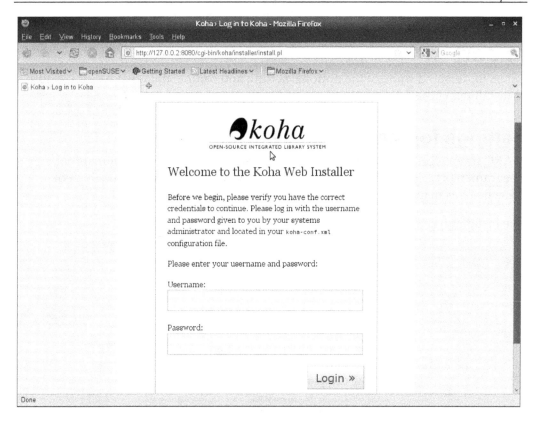

- The web installer is launched from the staff interface.

- We use a MySQL database user and password to login into the installer; this user must have privileges over Koha's database.

- Choosing the correct MARC flavor — MARC21 or UNIMARC is very important; it is not possible to change this configuration once the database is created.

- If you are evaluating or testing Koha, you should choose to import most or all of the optional settings and sample data. This way you can start using Koha right away.

- The optional settings and sample data can be deleted or edited from Koha's staff client at any time, but this can be significant amount of work.

- If you have made a mistake in the configuration settings and want to start over, simply drop and recreate Koha's database from the MySQL prompt; you will be able to launch the web installer once again.

Understanding optional data available for import

Let us understand some of the optional setting and sample data that we can choose to install using the web installer.

Settings for MARC frameworks

MARC frameworks define how data is captured for different types of material. The frameworks control things such as, which MARC fields are used, which of these fields is mandatory, or which fields are under authority control.

The installer has three sets of optional settings that we can import:

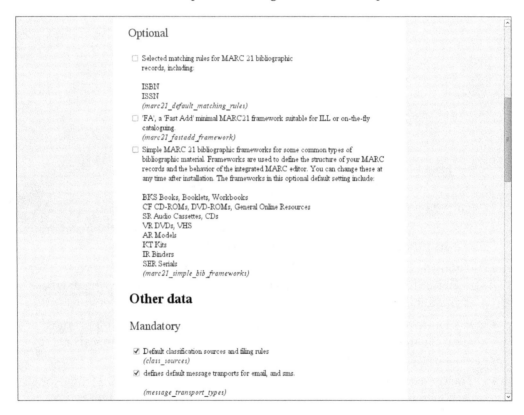

Optional

☐ Selected matching rules for MARC 21 bibliographic
records, including:

ISBN
ISSN
(marc21_default_matching_rules)

☐ 'FA', a 'Fast Add' minimal MARC21 framework suitable for ILL or on-the-fly
cataloguing.
(marc21_fastadd_framework)

☐ Simple MARC 21 bibliographic frameworks for some common types of
bibliographic material. Frameworks are used to define the structure of your MARC
records and the behavior of the integrated MARC editor. You can change these at
any time after installation. The frameworks in this optional default setting include:

BKS Books, Booklets, Workbooks
CF CD-ROMs, DVD-ROMs, General Online Resources
SR Audio Cassettes, CDs
VR DVDs, VHS
AR Models
KT Kits
IR Binders
SER Serials
(marc21_simple_bib_frameworks)

Other data

Mandatory

☑ Default classification sources and filing rules
(class_sources)
☑ defines default message tranports for email, and sms.

(message_transport_types)

- **Matching rules**: Matching rules are used during import of catalog records to match incoming records to those already in the database. Further action can be taken on matched records such as overwriting old records or adding holdings records. Two matching rules are available: one matches on ISBN and other on ISSN.

- **Fast Add framework**: This framework is designed for quickly adding catalog records; it has fewer fields when compared to other frameworks.

- **Simple MARC 21 Bibliographic frameworks**: A set of bibliographic frameworks for common types of material such as books, CDs, or serials.

Other data

Here is a listing of data we can import under the **Other data** section:

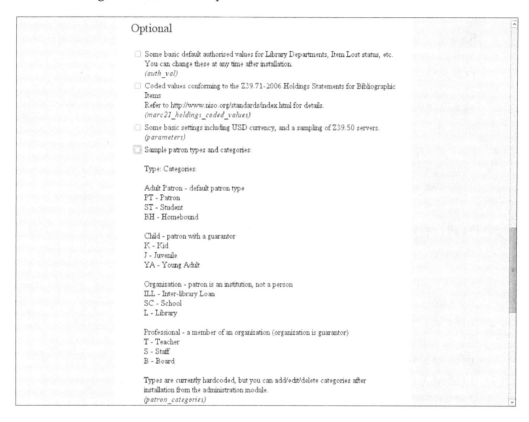

- **Authorized values**: Authorized values are lists of values that control data entry into catalog fields. Here we can import lists along with sample values for fields such as collections, shelving locations, or item statuses.

- **Currencies**: A set of currencies with sample exchange rates for use in Koha's Acquisitions module.

- **Sample patron types and categories**: A set of sample patron categories such as Student, Teacher, or Staff. Patron categories are used to define rules such as membership duration; the categories are also used to define circulation policy such as loan period.

- **Sample Label and Patron Card Data**: A set of sample layouts and templates for use in Koha's label and patron card generation, and printing tool.
- **Sample Holidays**: A sample set of holidays for use in Koha's calendar. The calendar is used in Koha's circulation module to calculate due dates and fines.
- **Default Item Types**: A sample set of item types. Item types are used to define circulation policy such as loan period or fine amount.
- **Sample Libraries**: A sample set of libraries, patrons, catalog items, circulation rules are linked to libraries.
- **Sample News Items**: A set of sample news items, for display on the OPAC and the staff interface.
- **Default messages or notices**: A set of sample notices. These are used in various Koha modules, for instance the Overdue notice can be configured to be sent to patrons with overdue items.
- **Sample Patrons**: A set of patron records.
- **Sample Z39.50 servers**: A sample set of Z39.50 servers such as that of the Library of Congress. These servers are used in Koha's cataloging module for copy catalog records into Koha.

Executing the web installer

Here are step-by-step instructions on executing the web installer:

1. Log in using the MySQL user and password; in this book we have used the user kohaadmin.
2. In Step 1, choose your language; you should see just one option here – en for English or fr for French.
3. In Step 2, the installer checks the database connectivity and user privileges.
4. In Step 3, the installer populates the database with tables before prompting the user to install basic configuration settings.
5. Select your MARC flavor – Unimarc or MARC 21. It is important to make the right choice here. Consult with your library staff if you are unsure of what to choose.
6. Choose to import optional data related to MARC frameworks.
7. Choose to import other optional data such as authorized values, currencies, or patron categories.
8. Click on **Import** to install the settings and sample data.
9. Choose to use Zebra or the regular database indexing.
10. Click on **Finish** to complete the execution of the web installer.

Launching Koha

Once the installer finishes it should automatically redirect to the staff interface:

Log in using the MySQL user and you should see Koha's staff interface home page:

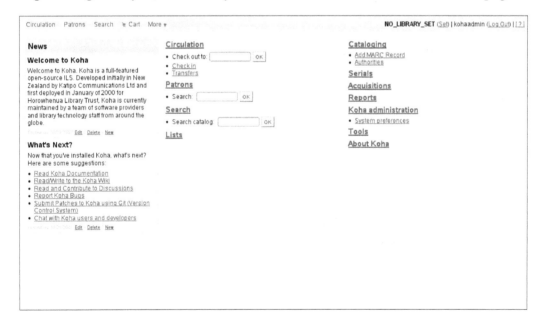

To launch the OPAC navigate to the OPAC url and you should see a screen such as this:

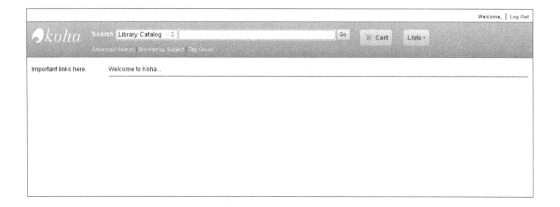

Configuring the crontab

Several Koha programs need to be run periodically. These programs calculate fines, generate overdue notices, send out e-mails, or build Zebra indexes.

We use Linux's Cron utility to schedule the execution of these programs.

Editing the crontab

The cronjobs are set up under the koha user's crontab. To edit the crontab we run the command `crontab` with the `-e` option:

```
koha@koha@linux:~> crontab -e
```

To save and exit, we use the vi command `wq`:

```
:wq
```

Setting up environment variables

The first thing we need to do is to set Koha related environment variables in the crontab; without these none of the cronjobs will execute. Add these lines in the crontab, somewhere at the top:

```
PERL5LIB=/home/koha/kohaclone
KOHA_CONF=/etc/koha-dev/etc/koha-conf.xml
```

Generating advance notices

Advance notices are sent to patrons when items are due. To generate such notices, we need to script advanced_notices.pl as a cronjob. Add a line to the crontab as follows:

```
49 5 * * * perl /home/koha/kohacone/bin/cronjobs/advance_notices.pl -c
```

This cronjob will execute at 5:49 AM every day and generate and queue advance notices messages to patrons.

Generating overdue notices

Overdue notices are sent to patrons when items are past due. To generate such notices, we need to script overdue_notices.pl as a cronjob. Add a line to the crontab as follows:

```
45 5 * * * perl /home/koha/kohaclone/bin/cronjobs/overdue_notices.pl -t
```

This cronjob will execute at 5:45 AM every day and generate and queue overdue notices messages to patrons.

Sending e-mail messages

To send e-mails to patrons we will need to script process_messages.pl in the crontab:

```
30 6 * * * perl /home/koha/kohaclone/bin/cronjobs/process_message_queue.pl
```

The process_messages.pl program sends out the queued messages via e-mail. This is the reason it should be scheduled after the advance notices and overdue notices cronjobs. In this example, we have scheduled the program to run at 6:30 AM every day.

Calculating fines

To calculate fines we script fines.pl as follows:

```
0 7 * * * perl /home/koha/kohaclone/bin/cronjobs/fines.pl
```

The fines.pl program calculates fines on overdue items based on circulation rules setup in Koha.

Rebuilding Zebra indexes

In *Chapter 3, Installing Koha's Zebra Search Engine*, we learned how to rebuild Zebra indexes by passing different parameters to the `rebuild_zebra.pl` program. To schedule index rebuilds, we script a cronjob as follows:

```
*/1 *  *   *   *  perl /home/koha/kohaclone/misc/migration_tools/rebuild_
zebra.pl -b -a -z >> /dev/null 2>&1
```

Note the following about this cronjob:

- The `*/1` at the beginning the cronjob signifies that the command will be executed every minute
- The output of the command is being redirected to the `/dev/null`, which means nowhere
- The expression `2>&1` means, that the command's error messages (2) and its standard output (1) will both be redirected to the same place, in this case `/dev/null`

To redirect the output and error messages to a log file, we setup the cronjob as follows:

```
*/1 *  *   *   *  perl /home/koha/kohaclone/misc/migration_tools/rebuild_
zebra.pl -b -a -z >> /home/koha/logs/zebra.log  2>&1
```

Note the use of the file `/home/koha/logs/zebra.log` instead of `/dev/null`.

More crontab examples

There are several other programs that can be set up in the crontab depending on your requirements. Take a look at the `/misc/cronjobs/crontab.example` file for more information:

```
koha@koha@linux:~> vi /home/koha/kohaclone/misc/cronjobs/crontab.example
```

Ensuring Koha starts automatically on server reboot

To make sure that Koha runs smoothly after a server reboot, we need to make sure that Apache2, MySQL, and Zebra server start up automatically. In this section, we demonstrate how to set this on Debian and openSuSE.

Auto-starting Apache2

On Debian, Apache2 is configured by default to start automatically on server reboot. In openSuSE, however, this is not the case. We use the chkconfig program to configure Apache2 to auto-start on reboot:

```
koha@koha@linux:~> sudo chkconfig apache2 on
```

Let us test if the command was successful; we run the command as follows:

```
koha@koha@linux:~> sudo chkconfig apache2
apache2   on
```

Auto-starting MySQL

Again on Debian, MySQL is already configured to start automatically on server reboot. In openSuSE, we use chkconfig to configure it to auto-start on reboot:

```
koha@koha@linux:~> sudo chkconfig mysql on
```

To test the configuration, we use chkconfig as follows:

```
koha@koha@linux:~> sudo chkconfig mysql
mysql   on
```

Auto-starting Zebra server

We need to configure the service koha-zebra-daemon to start up automatically on server reboot.

On Debian, we use the chkconfig equivalent command — update-rc.d to accomplish this:

```
koha@koha@linux:~> sudo update-rc.d koha-zebra-daemon defaults
```

On openSuSE, we use chkconfig as follows:

```
koha@koha@linux:~> sudo chkconfig koha-zebra-daemon on
```

On openSuSE, if you are not using the koha-zebra-daemon service, you can setup the zebrasrv command in the /etc/init.d/boot.local file.

Edit the boot.local file:

```
koha@koha@linux:~> sudo vi /etc/init.d/boot.local
```

Add the `zebrasrv` command to the file somewhere near the end of the file as follows:

```
# script with local commands to be executed from init on system startup
#
# Here you should add things, that should happen directly after booting
# before we're going to the first run level.
#
/usr/bin/zebrasrv -f /etc/koha-dev/etc/koha-conf.xml &
```

Note the use of the `&` character at the end of the `zebrasrv` command; this tells the command to run silently in the background.

Configuring the correct SAX parser

Koha uses Simple API for XML (SAX) parsers to process XML data. It is possible that multiple XML parsers are installed on the server. We need to use the `LibXML::SAX::Parser`. The other parsers such as `XML::SAX::PurePerl` or `XML::SAX::Expat` are known to have bugs with certain character types.

First we run a test to check which parser is setup on the server. To print the parser that is in use, we run the Koha program `/misc/sax_parser_print.pl`:

```
koha@koha@linux:~> cd /home/koha/kohaclone/misc/
koha@linux:/home/koha/kohaclone/misc # ./sax_parser_print.pl
Koha wants something like:
    XML::LibXML::SAX::Parser=HASH(0x81fe220)
You have:
    XML::LibXML::SAX=HASH(0x834fea4)
Looks bad, check INSTALL.* documentation.
```

That error, `looks bad`, indicates that the configured parser is not suitable for Koha use. We will need to edit the initialization file of the parser and change its configuration.

First we locate the file `ParserDetails.ini`:

```
koha@linux:/home/koha/kohaclone/misc # locate ParserDetails.ini
/usr/lib/perl5/vendor_perl/5.10.0/XML/SAX/ParserDetails.ini
```

We edit this file replace `[XML::SAX::PurePerl]` or `[XML::SAX::Expat]` as the case may be with `[XML::LibXML::SAX::Parser]`.

```
koha@linux:/home/koha/kohaclone/misc # cd
/usr/lib/perl5/vendor_perl/5.10.0/XML/SAX/

koha@linux:/usr/lib/perl5/vendor_perl/5.10.0/XML/SAX # vi ParserDetails.
ini
[XML::LibXML::SAX::Parser]
http://xml.org/sax/features/namespaces = 1
```

Let us test the parser configuration again; a correct file will result in an output like this:

```
koha@linux:/home/koha/kohaclone/misc # ./sax_parser_print.pl
Koha wants something like:
    XML::LibXML::SAX::Parser=HASH(0x81fe220)
You have:
    XML::LibXML::SAX::Parser=HASH(0x834fc94)
Looks good.
```

Setting up environment variables for the Linux shell

To run any of the Koha's programs from the Linux shell we need to set up up two environment variables properly – KOHA_CONF and PERL5LIB. Koha's Perl programs look at these variables to determine the location of the installation's configuration file – koha-conf.xml and the location of the application folder – kohaclone. In this section, we demonstrate how to setup these variables up for a single session and how to set these up to be persistent across sessions.

Setting up KOHA_CONF environment variable

The KOHA_CONF environment variable should point to Koha's configuration directory; in this book we have used /etc/koha-dev/etc/koha-conf.xml. To set up this variable, we use the export command:

```
koha@linux:/home/koha/kohaclone # export
KOHA_CONF=/etc/koha-dev/etc/koha-conf.xml
```

Let us test to make sure the variable is set correctly:

```
koha@libux:/home/koha/kohaclone # echo $KOHA_CONF
/etc/koha-dev/etc/koha-conf.xml
```

Setting up PERL5LIB environment variable

The PERL5LIB environment variable points to the kohaclone folder. To set up this variable, we use the export command as follows:

```
koha@linux:/home/koha/kohaclone# export PERL5LIB=/home/koha/kohaclone
```

Let us test to make sure the variable is set correctly:

```
koha@linux:/home/koha/kohaclone# echo $PERL5LIB
/home/koha/kohaclone
```

Setting up persistent environment variables

To make sure the variables are persistent across sessions, we will need to export these variables in a bash configuration file.

On Debian, we set these up in the /etc/bash.bashrc file:

```
koha@linux:/home/koha # vi /etc/bash.bashrc
```

On openSuSE, we use the /etc/bash.backrc.local file:

```
koha@linux:/home/koha # vi /etc/bash.bashrc.local
```

We add these lines to the file:

```
export KOHA_CONF=/etc/koha-dev/etc/koha-conf.xml
export PERL5LIB=/usr/share/kohaclone
```

To test if the configuration is successfully setup, we open a new terminal session and run the echo command:

```
koha@linux:~> echo $KOHA_CONF
/etc/koha-dev/etc/koha-conf.xml
koha@koha@linux:~> echo $PERL5LIB
/home/koha/kohaclone
koha@linux:~>
```

Summary

Here is what we learned in this chapter:

- Executing Koha's web installer to populate the database structure and mandatory administrative settings
- Configuring the crontab to schedule Koha's batch programs
- Configuring the necessary XML SAX parser
- Configuring Apache2, MySQL, and Zebra server to start automatically on reboot

We have now completed the installation and server configuration phase of the book. In the next set of chapters we will use Koha's staff interface to configure the various Koha modules. In the next chapter, we will configure the cataloging module.

5
Configuring the Cataloging Module

In this chapter, we will learn how to configure Koha's Cataloging module. This module is used to maintain information about items in the library. Cataloging is an important function—a good catalog helps patrons find and evaluate items easily.

Our goals in this chapter will be to:

- Make cataloging screens simpler to use
- Control the fields to prevent errors to bring about consistency and quality

To do this we will need to study three of Koha's cataloging configuration tools:

- **MARC Frameworks**
- **Authority Control**
- **Authorized values**

To configure these tools effectively we will need to first develop a configuration plan based on an understanding of the library's needs and circumstances.

A first look at Koha's cataloging configuration tools

Before we create our cataloging configuration plan let us understand Koha's configuration tools:

- MARC frameworks are cataloging templates for different types of material in the library

- Authority Control allows us to control data entry in certain fields. Authority Control is used for title, name, and subject fields

- Authorized values offer an additional way to control data entry. These are used mainly for item or local use fields.

MARC frameworks

Koha's MARC frameworks are a way to simplify catalog data entry, also to control what gets entered. Think of these as cataloging templates for different types of material in the library.

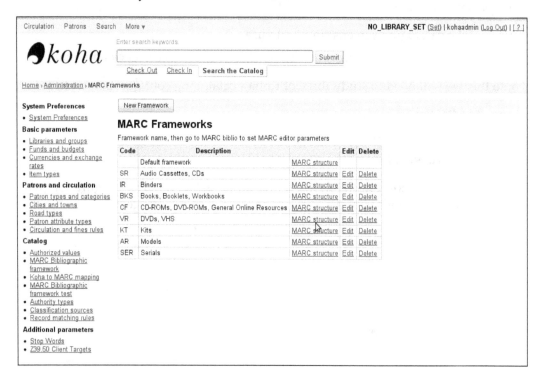

Here are some notes on frameworks:

- While installing Koha you can choose to install a set of frameworks for commonly used material types
- New frameworks can be created by modelling them on existing ones
- Frameworks can be edited or deleted at any time
- The default framework has a broad set of fields and can be used for material that doesn't fit into any other framework
- Frameworks control how a catalog record is entered and displayed in the cataloging screens
- Frameworks have no impact on records that are imported via Koha's import or Z39.50 copy cataloging tools

With MARC frameworks, for each type of material, we can define what fields and subfields are:

- Available for data entry
- Mandatory

To control data entry, we can also bring some of these fields or subfields under:

- Authority Control
- Authorized Values Control

Authority Control

Data entry into bibliographic fields can be controlled using Authority Control. Bibliographic cataloguers cannot enter text in fields under Authority Control; they can only pick values from the list of authority records.

This text from Wikipedia (`http://en.wikipedia.org/wiki/Authority_control`) describes the purpose of authority control well:

Authority control fulfils two important functions.

First, it enables catalogers to disambiguate items with similar or identical headings. For example, two authors who happen to have published under the same name can be distinguished from each other by adding middle initials, birth and/or death (or flourished, if these are unknown) dates, or a descriptive epithet to the heading of one (or both) authors.

Second, authority control is used by catalogers to collocate materials that logically belong together, although they present themselves differently. For example, authority records are used to establish uniform titles, which can collocate all versions of a given work together even when they are issued under different titles.

Authority records are usually created for name, title, and subject headings. Some bibliographic fields that are can be brought under authority control are:

- 100$a: Personal name
- 110$a: Corporate name
- 111$a: Meeting name
- 139$a: Uniform title
- 600$a: Subject: Personal name
- 610$a: Subject: Corporate name
- 611$a: Subject: Meeting name
- 650$a: Subject: Topic
- 651$a: Subject: Geographic name
- 655$a: Subject: Genre/Form

In Koha, Authority Control is implemented using:

- Authorities system preferences
- Authority types

Authorities related system preferences control:

- Whether Authority Control is used or not
- Whether new bibliographic records result in automatic creation of authority records
- Whether updates to authority records should update linked bibliographic records

Some key points on Authority Types are:

- Authority Types are MARC frameworks for authority headings
- While installing Koha you can choose to install a set of commonly used authority types
- New Authority Types can be created, these can be edited or deleted at any time

- Authority Types are mapped to fields in Bibliographic MARC frameworks
- Authority Types control how an authority record is entered and displayed in the authorities cataloging screens as shown in the following screenshot:

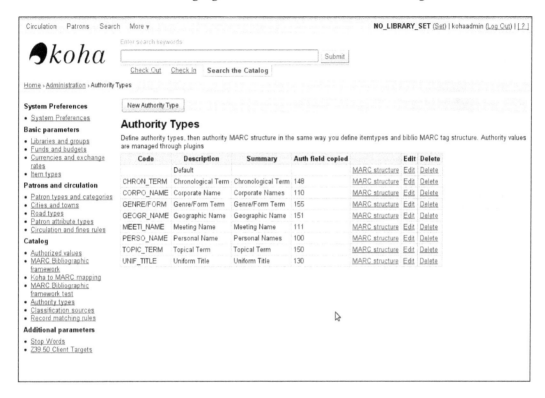

Authorized values

Koha provides an additional way to control data entry — authorized values. These are simple lists of values that can be linked to any bibliographic field or subfield.

Catalogers will not be able to enter free text in fields that are controlled via authorized values; they will only be able to pick values from a list. Like Authority Control, authorized values help reduce errors and bring about consistency in catalog records.

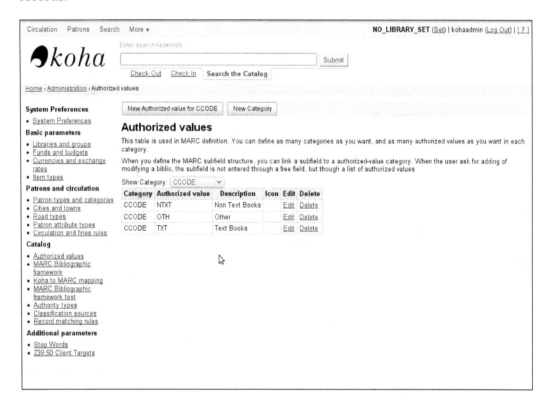

Item or Local use fields are usually controlled using authorized values. Some of these fields are:

- 952$2: Shelving scheme
- 952$8: Collection code
- 952$a: Home branch
- 952$c: Shelving location
- 952$j: Shelving control number
- 952$y: Item type

And here are some key points about authorized values:

- While installing Koha you can choose to install a set of commonly used authorized values categories along and corresponding values

- New Authority values categories and values can be created, edited, or deleted

- Authorized values categories can be mapped to fields in Bibliographic MARC frameworks

- Some authorized values such as branch and item type are special and they are configured under Koha's Administration screens

Preparing a configuration plan

Before we configure Koha's cataloging module, we will need to develop a plan based on the library's needs and circumstances. We will need to identify how to use Koha's Authority Control, what types of material we would want to catalog, and what fields and subfields we will need for each material type. We will also need to define which of these fields and subfields will be mandatory, which ones will be controlled using Authority Control or Authorized Values Control.

Identifying Authority Control rules

We will first need to decide how to use Koha's Authority Control, if at all.

Using Authority Control has cost implications; you will need staff to maintain your authority files, or you may outsource this work. You may have to purchase authority records from the Library of Congress or other sources.

You will also need to establish a process for using Authority Control. Will you create authority records during the creation of bibliographic records, or after? What process will you follow when authority headings are updated?

Based on this you can develop a plan that looks something like this:

Question	Plan
Use Authority Control?	Yes
Create authority records before bibliographic records are created, or after they are created	After bibliographic records are created
Do you want bibliographic records to be automatically updated when authority records are updated?	Yes

Identifying frequently cataloged types of material

Create a list of materials that are cataloged often and have distinct bibliographic characteristics, in terms of fields and subfields that are commonly used.

Our list might look something like this:

- Books
- Serials
- Visual materials
- Reports/Dissertations
- Electronic material

You will need to create a Bibliographic framework for each item in this list.

Identifying MARC field sets for each type of material

For each type of material above, we will list the fields and subfields that will be used during cataloging. For instance, for books, we might want a field set similar to this:

- 020: ISBN
- 082: Call number
- 1XX: Author fields
- 245: Title
- 260$a: Place of publication
- 260$b: Publisher

- 260$c: Date of publication
- 300: Physical description
- 500: General note
- 505: Formatted contents note
- 6XX: Various subject fields
- 7XX: Other authors
- 952$a: Home branch
- 952$d: Date acquired
- 952$p: Barcode
- 952$y: Item type

Identifying mandatory fields

Next, for each field and subfield we will indicate if it needs to be mandatory. If data for a certain field is always available, and the field helps patrons find or evaluate an item, it might be a good idea to make it mandatory. Our configuration plan for books now looks like this:

Tag/Subfield	Mandatory?
020: ISBN	No
082: Call number	No
1XX: Author fields	No
245: Title	Yes
260$a: Place of publication	Yes
260$b: Publisher	Yes
260$c: Date of publication	Yes
300: Physical description	Yes
500: General note	No
505: Formatted contents note	No
6XX: Various subject fields	Yes
7XX: Other authors	No
952$a: Home branch	Yes
952$d: Date acquired	Yes
952$p: Barcode	Yes
952$y: Item type	Yes

Identifying Authority Control rules

Here will need to decide which bibliographic fields will be under Authority Control. The usual name, title, and subject fields are natural choices, but you can consider other fields too.

Let us add an Authority Control column to our example:

Tag/Subfield	Mandatory?	Authority Control
020: ISBN	No	
082: Call number	No	
1XX: Author fields	Yes	Yes
245: Title	Yes	
260$a: Place of publication	Yes	
260$b: Publisher	Yes	Yes
260$c: Date of publication	Yes	
300: Physical description	Yes	
500: General note	Yes	
505: Formatted contents note	No	
6XX: Various subject fields	Yes	Yes
7XX: Other authors	No	Yes
952$a: Home branch	Yes	
952$d: Date acquired	Yes	
952$p: Barcode	Yes	
952$y: Item type	Yes	

Identifying fields to control using authorized values

Some fields such as branch and item type are controlled by default. Other fields that can be populated by short lists of fixed or infrequently changing values are also good candidates.

Let us add an authorized values control column to our example:

Tag/Subfield	Mandatory?	Authority Control	Authorized values control
020: ISBN	No		
082: Call number	No		
1XX: Author fields	Yes	Yes	
245: Title	Yes		
260$a: Place of publication	Yes		Yes
260$b: Publisher	Yes	Yes	
260$c: Date of publication	Yes		
300: Physical description	Yes		
500: General note	Yes		
505: Formatted contents note	No		
6XX: Various subject fields	Yes	Yes	
7XX: Other authors	No	Yes	
952$a: Home branch	Yes		Yes
952$d: Date acquired	Yes		
952$p: Barcode	Yes		
952$y: Item Type	Yes		Yes

This completes our configuration plan for books. You can create similar plans for other types of material.

Implementing our configuration plan

Now that we have a configuration plan in place, let us look at how to implement it in Koha. We will first setup Authority Control and authorized values and then use them in a new MARC framework.

Configuring authorities system preferences

We will need to set two system preferences:

- **BiblioAddsAuthorities:** Turn this **Off**, if you expect to have authority records available for use during creation of bibliographic records. If this is set to **On**, authority control is turned off; Catalogers can enter the data in the field, and Koha automatically creates authority records based on what is entered in the corresponding bibliographic field.

- **dontmerge:** Set this to **On**, if you want linked bibliographic records to be automatically updated when an authority records is updated.

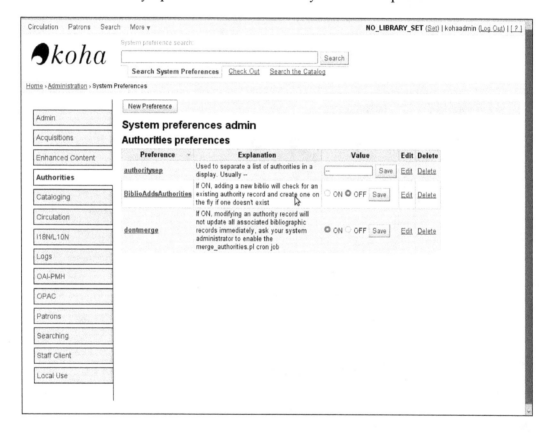

To edit these preferences, navigate to **Administration | Global system preferences**. Search for the system preference by its name to find it.

Configuring Authority Types

Authority Types are MARC frameworks for authority records. Commonly used Authority Types are available with the default installation of Koha. You can create new ones if you want to bring fields other than name and subject headings under Authority Control.

To create a new authority type, follow these steps:

1. We find **Authority Types** screens in the **Catalog** section under **Administration**.

2. Click on **New Authority Type** button.

3. Enter an Authority Type code, **Description**, and **Summary**.

4. The field **Authority field to copy** is most important we enter the tag in the authority record that should be copied into the bibliographic record. Look at the existing Authority Types for reference.

Configuring authorized values categories

We will need an authorized values category for each field we want to control using authorized values.

Find **Authorized Values** screens in the Catalog section under **Administration**. The pre-configured set of categories is listed in the **Show Category** list of values.

To create new categories, we use the **New Category** button.

Editing authorized values

To edit the list of values in a category, we first select the category from the **Show category** list of values.

We use the button **New Authorized value for <Category Name>** to create new values.

Special authorized values

Some authorized values categories are maintained in the **Administration** section directly. We'll look at these now:

Library

Libraries can be maintained in **Libraries and groups** section in the **Basic parameters** section under **Administration**.

Item Type

Item Types can be maintained in **Item Types** n the **Basic parameters** section under **Administration**.

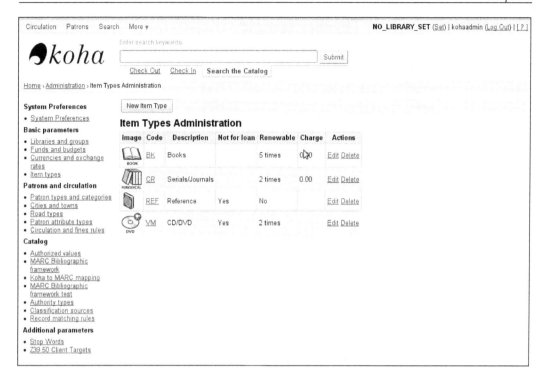

Configuring MARC frameworks

Now that we have Authority Types and Authorized Values Categories set up, let us look at editing our MARC framework list, and configuring the fields and subfields in a framework.

Editing MARC framework list

We use the **New Framework** button to create, the **Edit** link to edit, and the **Delete** link to delete frameworks.

Key points to remember:

- Try not to edit or delete any preconfigured frameworks, at least initially
- Create new frameworks, Koha allows you to model new frameworks on existing ones
- Only once your own frameworks are fully ready, should you consider consider removing the preconfigured ones
- You should retain the default framework for material types that have no frameworks

Creating a new framework

To create a new framework, we use the **New Framework** button. Once the **Framework Code** and **Description** is saved, we click on the **MARC structure** link.

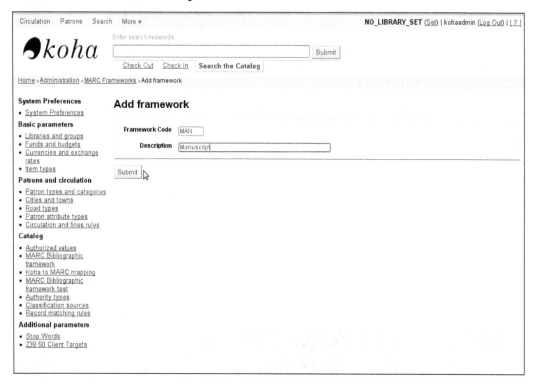

At this stage, we choose an existing framework as a model for the new one. Choosing the right framework in this step will save a lot of effort.

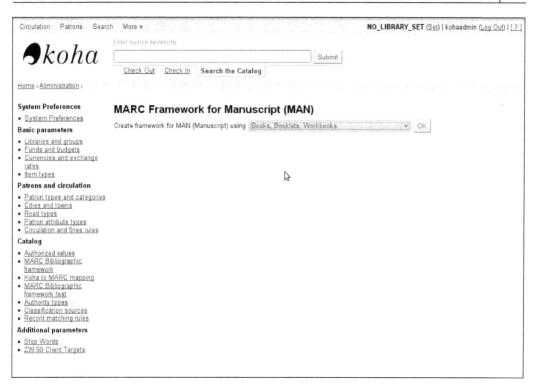

Editing fields and subfields

Let us now edit the fields and subfields in the new framework.

Remember that Bibliographic tags are numbered from 0XX through 8XX. Item or local use data is stored in tag 952.

Use the **Search for tag** feature to navigate to the field you wish to edit. Use the **Display only used Tags/Subfields** checkbox as a navigation aid.

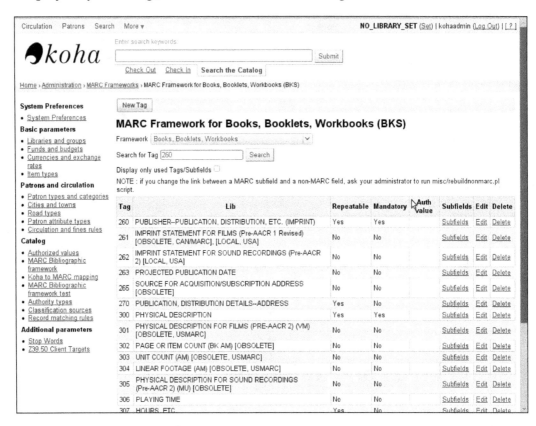

To edit the field, click on **Edit**. To edit subfields click on **Subfields**, and click on the **Edit Subfields** button at the bottom of the page.

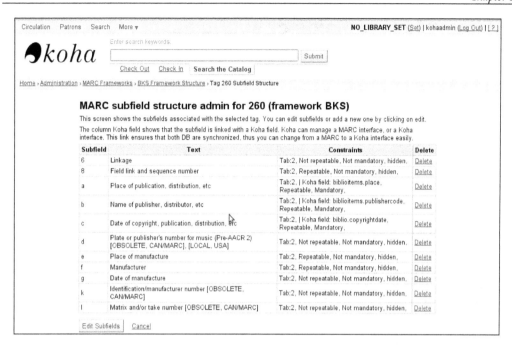

Navigate to the specific subfield you wish to edit by clicking on the appropriate tab at the top.

Editing labels of fields or subfields

To edit how a tag or subfields is labeled in the cataloging screens, edit the field **Text for librarians**.

Making a field or subfield mandatory

To make a tag or subfield mandatory simply check the box **Mandatory** in the **Basic Constraints** block.

Advanced constraints

Click on the link **Display more constraints** below the **Basic constraints** block to display **Advanced constraints**.

Hidden fields and subfields

This field controls if a tag or subfield is displayed in the MARC editor, and if yes, in what form—collapsed or not.

The field can have several values, for the purposes of cataloging; you will need to learn these:

- 0: Displayed, not collapsed
- -1: Displayed, collapsed
- -2: Not displayed

Bringing fields or subfields under Authorized Value or Authority Control

You can bring the field under Authorized Values control OR under Authority Control. It does not make sense to use both.

To use Authorized Values, select the appropriate Category from the **Authorized value** list of values.

To use Authority Control, select the appropriate type from the **Thesaurus** list of values.

Summary

In this chapter, we used three tools to make cataloging simpler and to control data entry:

- **MARC Frameworks**
- **Authority Control**
- **Authorized values**

Developing an effective configuration plan in advance is important.

There are cost implications to using Authority Control. You will need to incorporate your process of using Authority Control in the configuration plan.

You will need to develop a MARC framework for each material type that you catalog frequently, for the rest you can use the default framework. Within each framework you will need to configure which fields and subfields are available, and which of those are mandatory. Some of the fields can be brought under Authority Control; others may be controlled using authorized values.

In the next chapter, *Configuring the Circulation Module*, we will learn how to map the library's circulation policies to rules and preferences in Koha.

6
Configuring the Circulation Module

In this chapter, we will learn how to configure Koha's circulation module. This module is used to loan library items to the patrons. Our goal will be to map the library's circulation policies to rules and preferences in Koha.

A library's circulation policies govern loan periods, renewals, membership duration, fines, holds, reference material, and so on.

To map these in Koha, we will study the following Koha features:

- Patron categories
- Item types
- Circulation and fine rules
- Notices and triggers
- Calendar
- Circulation system preferences

Patron categories

We create a patron category for each group or class of patrons that has distinct characteristics or needs.

Patron categories are a very important part of Koha's circulation module.

You can find the Patron Category Administration screen in the **Patrons and Circulation** section in Koha's **Administration** module.

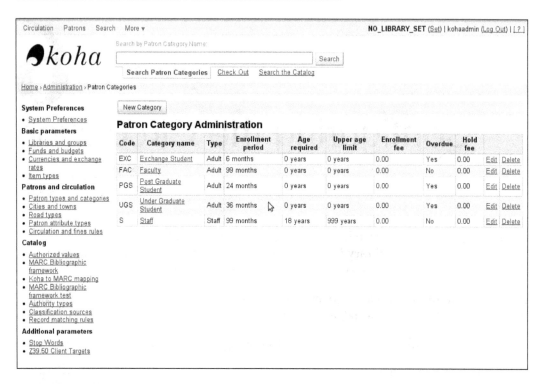

Identifying patron categories

Unless your library is just starting up, you will already have your list of patron categories. However, you might consider modifying the list to take advantage of some of Koha's capabilities.

The key question here is do you have, or anticipate groups of patrons that have distinct characteristics. We need to assess if these groups are different in one or more of following ways:

- Enrolment duration
- Enrolment fee
- Age restrictions
- Loan periods
- Maximum checkouts allowed
- Fine amounts

Here are some examples for different types of libraries:

- Public library: In a public library, these categories might be suitable:
    ◦ Adult
    ◦ Child
    ◦ Student
    ◦ Staff
    ◦ Institution
- Academic library: In an academic library, these categories might be suitable:
    ◦ Under graduate student
    ◦ Post graduate student
    ◦ Faculty
- Commercial library: In a commercial library, you might create categories like these:
    ◦ Plan A: Rs. 250 a month
    ◦ Plan B: Rs. 500 a month
    ◦ Plan C: Rs. 1,000 a month

Creating patron categories

To create a new category we use the **New Category** button. Use this table as a guide to create or edit patron categories:

Field	Mandatory?	Instructions	Comments
Category Code	Yes	Enter short code for the category, for example, UGS.	
Description	Yes	Enter description of category, for example, under graduate Student.	
Enrolment Period	No	Enter enrolment period in months.	Field used to autocalculate membership expiry date.
Age Required	No	Enter lower age limit.	

Field	Mandatory?	Instructions	Comments
Upper Age Limit	No	Enter upper age limit.	
Enrolment Fee	No	Enter fee amount.	This fee will be charged when first enrolled.
Overdue Notice Required	No	Select or deselect the checkbox.	Controls if due and overdue notices will be sent to patrons of this category.
Hold Fee	No	Enter Fee Amount.	This fee will be charged every time a patron of this category places a hold on an item.
Category Type	Yes	Choose from list of values.	Child: requires an adult guarantor. Staff: have additional privileges, only for library staff .

Item types

Item types are groups of items of material in the library that are circulated in different ways.

Item types are also a very important part of Koha's circulation module.

You can find the types screen in the **Patrons and Circulation** section in Koha's **Administration** module.

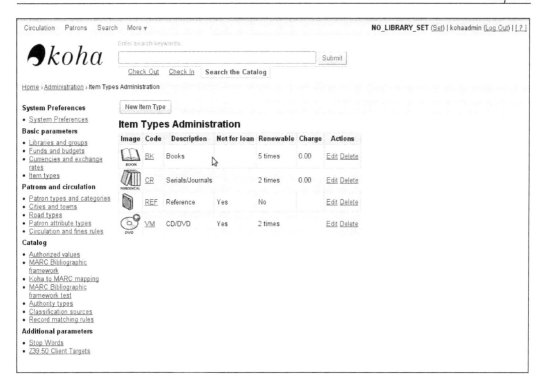

Identifying Item types

Unless your library is just starting up, you will already have your list of Item types. Just like with patron categories you might consider modifying the item type list to take advantage of some of Koha's capabilities.

We will need to consider what types of material in the library have have distinct characteristics. We need to assess if types of material are different in one or more of following ways:

- Renewal policies
- Not for loan policies
- Loan period
- Maximum checkouts
- Fine amount
- Rental charge

Here's a good example of Koha's default Item type list:

- Books
- Reference
- Journals
- Reports
- CD/DVDS

Creating Item types

To create a new item type we use the **New Item Type** button. Use this table as a guide to create or edit an item type:

Field	Mandatory?	Instructions	Comments
Item Type	Yes	Enter short code for the category, for example, BK	
Description	Yes	Enter description of item type, for example, Books	
Images	No	Choose image from available list or provide a URL to a image on an external server	
Not for Loan	No	Select or deselect the checkbox	If this option is checked, items of this type cannot be checked out.
Renewals	No	Enter number	Number will indicate maximum number of renewals possible on items of this type. Leave blank or enter 0 to indicate no renewals allowed.
Rental Charge	No	Enter rental charge amount	Amount will be charged each time an item of this type is checked out.
Summary	No	Enter free text	

Circulation and fine rules

In Koha, for a combination of library or branch, patron category and item type, you can specify:

- Loan period
- Fine amount
- Maximum checkouts

In addition, for a combination of library or branch and patron category, you can also specify:

- Maximum checkouts

The second type of rule is used to constrain the total number of checkouts across all item types.

You can find the **Circulation and Fine Rules** screens in the **Patrons and Circulation** section under Koha's **Administration** module.

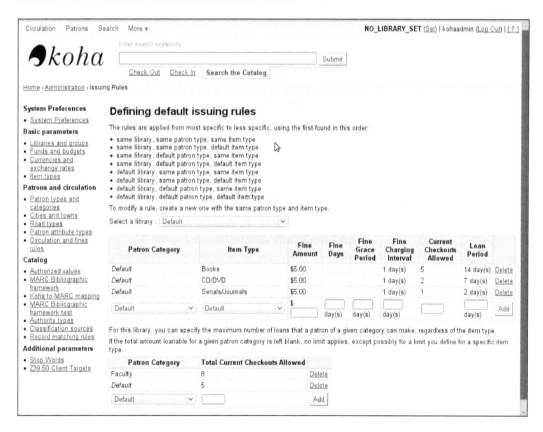

Identifying circulation and fine rules

Unless your library is just starting up, you will already have your list of circulation and fine rules. However, you might consider modifying the list to take advantage of some of Koha's capabilities.

Based on your current circulation and fine policies, record data in a table in the following fashion:

Library or branch	Patron category	Item Type	Loan Period	Fine Amount	Current Checkout Allowed
Library A	Student	Books	21	5	5
Library B	Student	Books	21	5	5
Library C	Student	Books	14	10	3
Library A	Student	CDs	21	5	5
Library B	Student	CDs	21	5	5
Library C	Student	CDs	14	10	3

And this table as well:

Library or Branch	Patron Category	Total Current Checkouts Allowed
Library A	Student	5
Library B	Student	5
Library C	Student	5

Creating circulation and fine rules

If you take all combinations of library or branch, patron category and item type the number of rules to configure and maintain would be very large.

Thankfully, Koha allows us to use the value "Default" to denote all values. This way you need to configure a small number of default rules and another small number of rules for exceptions.

This is best explained using the example in the previous section. The example we just saw can be translated to following rules for Koha:

Library or branch	Patron category	Item Type	Loan Period	Fine Amount	Current Checkout Allowed
Default	Student	Default	21	5	5
Library C	Student	Default	14	10	3

The first rule above can apply to Library C as well; however Koha will use the second rule for Library C, as it is more specific.

Similarly the total current checkout table can be configured as follows:

Library or branch	Patron category	Total Current Checkouts Allowed
Default	Default	5

Configuring the calendar and calculation of due date and fines

In this section we will learn about Koha's **calendar** module and how to configure **fines** and **due date** calculations.

Koha holidays
It is important to note that in Koha, a holiday is any day when the library is closed.

Calendar and fine calculation

You can choose to have Koha ignore the **Calendar**. If the calendar is ignored **fines** are calculated every day, even if the day is a holiday.

Calculation of due dates in Koha

Koha offers three options for **due date** calculations:

- You can choose to have Koha ignore the calendar; the due date will be calculated as check out date plus loan period, even if this date is a holiday.

- You can have Koha exclude holidays from the loan period. So in this case the due date will be calculated as check out date plus loan period plus number of holiday during loan period.

- If you have Koha include holidays in the loan period, the due date will be calculated as checkout date plus loan period, if this date falls on a holiday, Koha will move the due date forward to the next working day.

Preparing to configure the calendar and fines and due date calculations

Before we can start the configuration, you will need to gather this information:

- Holiday list for the year
- Whether Saturdays are holidays
- Whether Sundays are holidays
- Your library's policy on fines calculation with regards to holidays
- Your library's policy on due date calculation with regards to holidays

Editing the calendar

The calendar module is available in the **Tools** section.

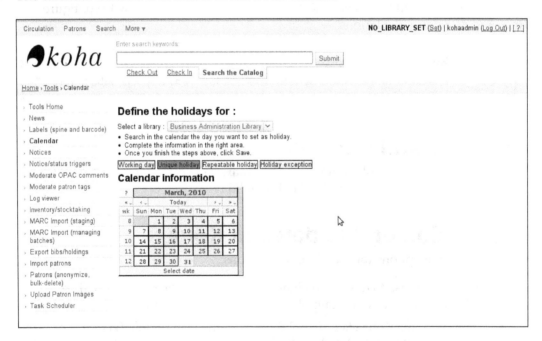

To configure the calendar, we follow these steps:

1. If Sundays are holidays, click on the nearest Sunday in the calendar and choose option **Holiday repeated every same day of the week**.

2. If Saturdays are holidays, click on the nearest Saturday in the calendar and choose options **Holiday repeated every same day of the week**.

3. For holidays that repeat every year on the same date (for example, Christmas), click on the date and choose option **Holiday repeated yearly on the same date**.

4. For other holidays, click on the date and choose the option **Holiday only on this day**.

Editing system preferences

There are three **System Preferences** you will need to set:

*   **finesmode**

    ◦   Set this to production; without this Koha will not accrue fines.

*   **finesCalendar**

    ◦   Choose **noFinesWhenClosed** if you don't want fines to accrue on holidays.

    ◦   Choose **ignoreCalendar** if you want fines to accrue on holidays.

*   **useDaysMode**

    ◦   Choose **Calendar** if you want due date to be check out date plus loan period plus number of holidays during loan period.

    ◦   Choose **Days** if you want due date to be checkout date plus loan period. Holidays are ignored.

    ◦   Choose **Datedue** if you want due date to be check out date plus loan period. Due date is moved forward only if it falls on a holiday.

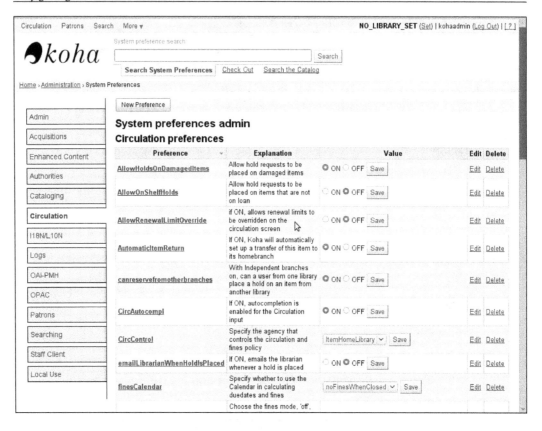

Due and overdue notices

Koha can automatically generate and e-mail due and overdue notices.

We will need to define:

- **Templates**: Text to be included in the notices, along with fields that will be populated dynamically
- **Triggers**: Definitions of when each type of notice should be sent for each patron category

Preparing to configure due and overdue notices

To configure due and overdue notices, we will need to prepare a plan. We will need to identify which patron categories will receive notices, how many notices will be sent and when, and what the content will be in each notice. Our plan may look like this:

Patron category	First notice		Second notice		Third notice	
	Delay	Template	Delay	Template	Delay	Template
Exchange Student	1	Item Due Reminder	3	Overdue Notice 1	5	Overdue Notice 2
Under Graduate Student	1	Item Due Reminder	3	Overdue Notice 1	5	Overdue Notice 2
Post Graduate Student	1	Item Due Reminder	3	Overdue Notice 1	5	Overdue Notice 2

For each template in the plan, we will need to prepare the text:

- Item due reminder
- Item overdue notice 1
- Item overdue notice 2

Editing notices

The **Notices** screen can be found in the **Tools** section. The following screenshot shows the notices templates:

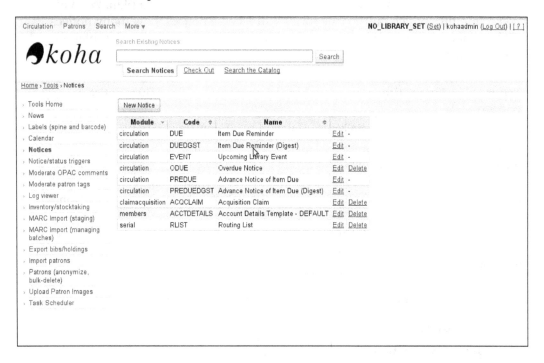

To create a new notice or template we use the button **New Notice**, and to edit an existing notice we use the **Edit** link.

We write the text of the notice in the **Message Body**. Some content, such as a borrower's name, will be dynamically populated by Koha when the notices are e-mailed to patrons. You can select the fields that you want from the box on the left. Use the **>>** button to move the selected fields into the message body.

Once notice templates are created, we can configure notice triggers.

Editing notice triggers

Notice triggers screens can be found in the **Tools** section. Here we configure, for each patron category when each notice should be e-mailed.

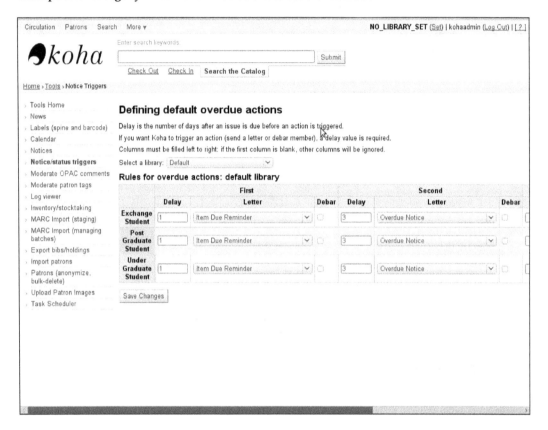

For each patron category define the delay and the template to be used in the first, second, and third letter boxes.

Some points to note:

- If you don't see a patron category listed in the screen, you will need to edit that patron category from the **Administration** section, and select the checkbox **Overdue Notice Required**.

- You do not need to have all three letters configured.

- If you don't configure any letters, notices will be not be sent out for that patron category.

- If you do need notices to be sent out, make sure you have the first letter configured properly.

Configuring holds

Replace this with "Finally, let us turn our attention to holds. Using Koha's holds feature, patron can request that certain items be reserved for them. Holds are usually placed on items that checked out. Once an item is placed on hold for a patron, the patron needs to pick up the item from the library within a specified number of days failing which the hold is cancelled and the item is made available for circulation.

We configure holds in Koha using system preferences."

Preparing to configure holds

Based on your library reserves or holds policy, you should prepare a plan such as this:

Reserves policy	Value
Maximum number of holds per patron	5
Maximum delay in picking up an item on hold	7
Whether to allow holds on items not on loan	No
Number of days before a hold is cancelled	7
Maximum fee or fine amount outstanding before ability to place holds is blocked	50
Whether to allow patron of one library to request a hold on an item in another library	No

Editing holds preferences

Most of the holds related **System preferences** are in the **Circulation** tab. You can also search for these using words **hold** or **reserve**.

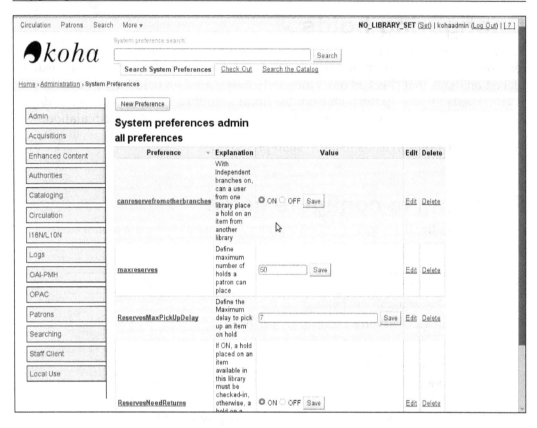

Here is a complete list of preferences:

- **AllowHoldsOnDamagedItems**
- **AllowOnShelfHolds**
- **canreservefromotherbranches**
- **emailLibrarianWhenHoldIsPlaced**
- **holdCancelLength**
- **maxoutstanding**
- **maxreserves**
- **RandomizeHoldsQueueWeight**
- **ReservesMaxPickUpDelay**
- **ReservesNeedReturns**
- **StaticHoldsQueueWeight**

Summary

Circulation is arguably the most important function in a library. In this chapter, we learned:

- How to map a library's policies to Koha's rules and system preferences.
- Patron categories control enrolment duration, age restrictions, and circulation and fine policies for different groups of patrons.
- Item types control renewals, not for loan, and circulation and fine policies for different types of material in the library.
- Koha's circulation and fines rules configuration module is used to set loan period, maximum checkout, and fine rules for combinations of patron categories, item types, and libraries or branches.
- You will help yourself by learning how to keep the number of rules to a small number using "Default" values.
- Holds are controlled mainly via system preferences. The preferences control among other things maximum reserves per patron, maximum duration before a reserve is cancelled, and the maximum delay in picking up an item on hold.

In the next chapter, our last on application configuration, we learn how to configure system preferences related to acquisitions, serials, the OPAC, and the staff client.

7
Configuring Other System Preferences

In this chapter, our goal will be to complete the application configuration and be in a position to use Koha in a test or production environment. We will learn to configure system preferences related to:

- The rest of the transactional modules — patrons, acquisitions, and serials
- The Online Public Access Catalog (OPAC)
- Styling and appearance of the OPAC and the staff client
- Messaging, security, and search

Koha has dozens of system preferences, some more important than others. We will focus on the important ones in this chapter. Readers should refer to Koha's online user manual for latest information on other preferences.

Understanding Koha's system preferences

System preferences are essentially choices that each Koha library makes about how the Koha should function. In this first section of the chapter, let us learn about Koha's system preferences module, the nature, and organization of the preferences. We share tips on using these preferences and finding information on these online.

Koha's global system preferences module

The **Global system preferences** module can be found under **Koha Administration**.

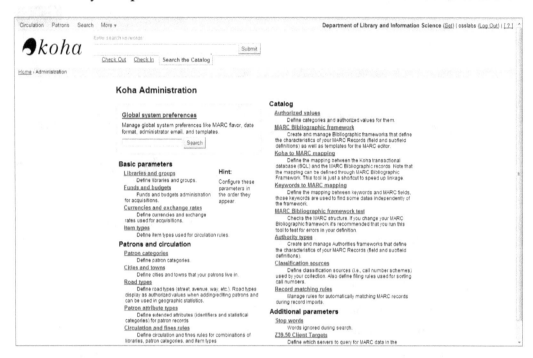

Here are the key points to note about this module:

- There are several dozen preferences, and these are organized by categories.

- These preference control system behavior such as whether budgets will be used in Acquisitions, or whether the patron card number will be auto-calculated.

- A handy search tool is available to find specific preferences.

- Preferences are of many types, from simple on/off switches to more complex list of values.

- Many preferences have default values set. You can change the values at any time.

- Some system preferences are set based upon choices you made during Koha's installation.

Using system preferences

Here are some key points to note about using these preferences:

- These preferences apply to the whole system; it is not possible to have different choices for different libraries, patron categories, or other types of divisions with your library.

- Access to system preferences should be controlled. Changes to these preferences can significantly alter system behavior.

- You will probably want to set a few preferences when you start using the system, especially those related to cataloging, patrons, or circulation.

- System preferences can be changed at any time, as you become familiar with the system over time you can set other preferences to tailor Koha to your needs.

Online documentation

We will not be able to cover all the preferences in this chapter or other places in this book. Besides, system preferences change, new ones are added all the time, some preferences are deprecated or their categorization or values may change. Refer to Koha's online user manual for the latest information.

The Koha 3.0 user manual is here:

```
http://koha.org/documentation/manual/3.0/administration/global-
system-preferences/.
```

And the Koha 3.2 manual is here:

```
http://koha-community.org/documentation/3-2-manual/.
```

Configuring transactional modules

In earlier chapters we have learned how to configure cataloging and circulation. In this section we learn about system preferences that control the functioning of some of the other transactional modules—patrons, acquisitions, and serials modules:

- Patrons preferences control how patrons' records are created
- Acquisitions preferences relate to budgeting and taxes
- Serials preferences relate to routing lists, subscriptions renewals, and display of subscription history

Configuring patrons preferences

Let us start by learning about patrons-related system preferences. These preferences can be found under the **Patrons** tab.

The Patrons module is as important as Cataloging or Circulation because a library cannot function without patron records.

Some of the functions of the module are to:

- Categorize patrons
- Capture useful information about them
- Generate unique identifiers for each patron to use in circulation

We have already learnt about creating patron categories in earlier chapters. The following preferences help manage patron records:

System preference	System preferences tab	Description	Default values	Instructions
BorrowerMandatoryField	Patrons	Mandatory fields when creating a patron record	**zipcode| surname| cardnumber**	It is important to pay attention to this preference. Ensure that fields that you will need, e-mail address for instance, are made mandatory. This way you will not have to correct patron records at a later date. Add fields separated by "|". Fields are column names in database table "borrowers". To look up the names log on to mysql and describe the borrowers table. `mysql> desc borrowers;`
ExtendedPatronAttributes	Patrons	Create new attribute fields for patrons	Off	Set up patron attributed in section **Patron Attribute Types** under block **Patrons and Circulation** under **Koha Administration**.

System preference	System preferences tab	Description	Default values	Instructions
autoMemberNum	Patrons	Whether to auto calculate the patron number	On	Koha generates a running sequence of numbers. If you wish to generate card numbers outside of Koha turn this preference Off. If you don't turn this off, in some cases you may forget to populate the external number, and Koha will record the default auto generated number for this patron.
borrowerRelationship	Patrons	Relationships between guarantee and guarantor, used for Child patron type.	**father | mother**	Enter names separated by " | ". This set of values becomes available for selection in the Guarantor field when creating a patron record of type **Child**.

System preference	System preferences tab	Description	Default values	Instructions
memberofinstitution	Patrons	Whether patrons can be linked to Institutions	Off	Turn this preference On, to link patrons of type **Professionals** to specific institutions.
				You will need to set up a patron category for institutions, and then create patron records for various institutions.
				When adding a patron record for type **Professional**, you will be able to select such institutions to link to the patron.
patronimages	Patrons	Whether to allow use of patron images	Off	Turn this off if you have privacy concerns or don't want to store images on the server due to disk space constraints.

Configuring acquisitions preferences

Koha's Acquisitions module is used to acquire Library items, usually through purchases. Koha's acquisitions module allows:

- Creation of vendors and budgets
- Management of purchase suggestions
- Creation of orders
- Receipt of ordered items

- Tracking of late or missing orders
- Generation of claim letters

Unlike Cataloging and Circulation, relatively fewer libraries use Koha's Acquisitions module, instead they prefer to manage the process manually or on some other system.

Perhaps for this reason, Koha's Acquisitions module is a simple module and has few system preferences. These preferences can be found under the **Acquisitions** tab.

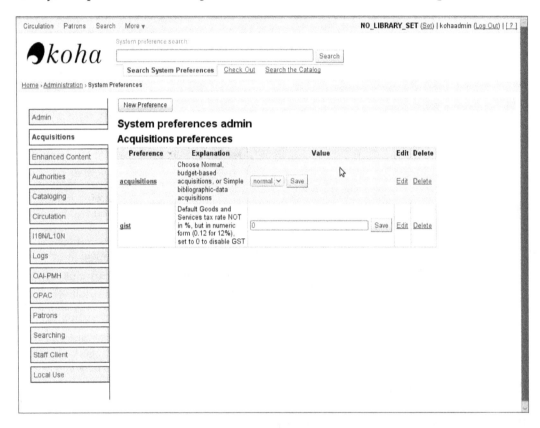

Here is an explanation of the Acquisitions preferences with instructions on how to configure them:

System preference	System preferences tab	Description	Default value	Instructions
acquisitions	Acquisitions	Whether to use budgets or not	normal	Set to "normal" to use budgets. Set to "simple" to make acquisitions without budgets.
emailPurchaseSuggestions	Acquisitions	Whether to have purchase suggestions e-mailed to the Koha admin or to use the **Manage suggestions** module within Koha	Off	Turn "On" to use e-mail. The e-mail will be sent to the e-mail address set up for the system preference **KohaAdminEmail Address**.
gist	Acquisitions	Defaults Goods and Services Tax Rate	0	"0" means GST is disabled. To use GST set to a numeric value, for example. 0.12 for 12%.

Configuring serials preferences

Koha's Serials module is used to manage subscriptions to periodicals. The module is used to:

- Create subscriptions with start dates and frequencies
- Receive issues when they arrive at the library
- Track missing or late issues
- Track renewals of subscription
- Generate claim letters for missing or late issues
- Maintain routing lists to notify specific patrons when new issues are received at the library

Like Acquisitions, relatively fewer libraries use this simple module, and there are fewer system preferences here as well.

In version 3.02 there is no serials or subscriptions category. You can find related system preferences by searching for the term *subscriptions*.

Here is an explanation of the Serials preferences with instructions on how to configure them:

System preference	System preferences tab	Description	Default value	Additional information
RoutingSerials	Cataloging	Whether to turn on routing lists	On	With this preference On, you can setup routing lists in Serials subscriptions. Routing lists are ordered set of names that each issue should be circulated to.

System preference	System preferences tab	Description	Default value	Additional information
RenewSerialAddsSuggestion	Serials	Whether to add a new purchase suggestion when renewing a serial	Off	Turn this on, if you want a way to remind the acquisition staff to renew the subscription with the vendor. A new purchase suggestion will be listed in the **Manage suggestions** module under **Acquisitions**. With this preference Off, the subscription will get renewed in Koha, but you will need to manually ensure that it is indeed renewed with the vendor.
SubscriptionHistory	Serials	The default subscription history view in the OPAC— simplified or full	Simplified	Turn to full if you want to show a full listing of the subscription history in the OPAC by default.

Configuring OPAC preferences

Koha's Online Public Access Catalog (OPAC) is not just an online catalog; it is also a self service tool for the patrons. Patrons can use the Koha OPAC to:

- Find items by entering search terms or by browsing categories
- Select items based on descriptions, ratings, reviews, and other useful material
- Place holds on items that are not available at the time
- Renew items they have borrowed
- Make purchase suggestions
- Review their borrowings, reading history, or fines
- Request changes to their address and other personal information
- Create and share reading lists
- Learn about library policies or upcoming events or News

Koha offers an extensive set of OPAC preferences that control:

- The static content on OPAC home page, from the page header to the content in the main block of the home page
- Tools that help patrons find, select, and manage their borrowings, such as virtual shelves or listing of most popular items
- Enhanced content that help patron select items, from Google jackets to Amazon reviews
- Patron access to features such as place holds or renew items

Configuring static content

We first configure the static content on the OPAC—the page header and footer, the content in the main body, the navigation bar, and the logo.

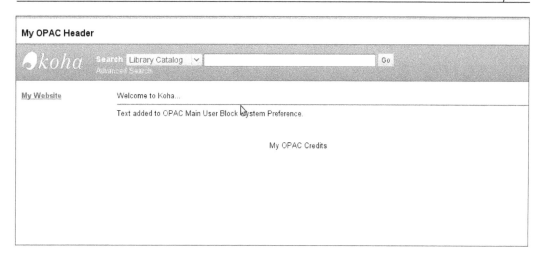

These preferences allow us to change OPAC content without having to edit the files on the server. It will help to have some HTML skills to maintain this set of preferences. With HTML you can format the content with color, emphasis, fonts, and font sizes.

Here is an explanation of these preferences with instructions on how to configure them:

System preference	System preferences tab	Description	Default value	Instructions
LibraryName	OPAC	Name that appears in the browser's title bar		Enter your Library's name, something like: Tailorbird Children's Library.
opaccredits	OPAC	Contents at the bottom of the OPAC page		Enter HTML contents, something like: `<p style="text-align:center"> My OPAC Credits</p>`

System preference	System preferences tab	Description	Default value	Instructions
opacheader	OPAC	Contents at the top of the OPAC page		Enter HTML contents, something like: `<h3>Welcome to my library</h3>`
OpacMainUserBlock	OPAC	Contents in the middle of OPAC home page	`Welcome to Koha... <hr>`	Enter HTML contents.
OpacNav	OPAC	Contents in the navigation block to the left of the page in the OPAC	Important links here.	Enter HTML contents, something like: `<a href="www.mywebsite.com">My Website</a>`
opacsmallimage	OPAC	Web URL of an image to replace default logo in the OPAC		Enter full path of the logo, something like: `http://mysite.com/logos/logo.png` Logo's size should be 120px*40px or less.

Configuring tools for patrons

Koha's OPAC has several tools that help patrons find, select, and manage items they want to borrow. These tools include — Browse by Subject, Listing of most popular items, virtual shelves, or reading lists, Book bag or cart, and a tool to allow online browsing of shelves.

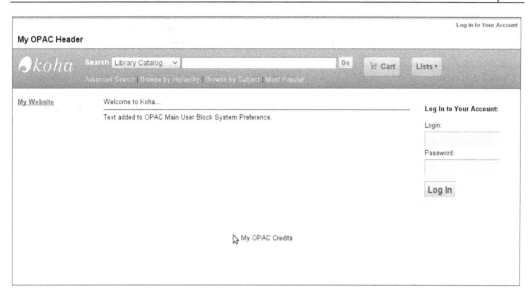

Here are the preferences along with instructions on how to use them:

System preference	System preferences tab	Description	Default value	Instructions
OpacAuthorities	OPAC	Whether to display "Browse by Subject" link below the Search box on the OPAC	On	This will allow you to search the Authorities records. This will work when you have authority records entered and indexed in the system.
opacbookbag	OPAC	Whether to display the "cart" or book bag in the mast head of the OPAC	On	The cart feature allows users to maintain a list of they want to borrow and also e-mail the list out. You will need to configure a mail server to send the e-mail out.

System preference	System preferences tab	Description	Default value	Instructions
OpacTopissue	OPAC	Whether to display the "Most Popular" link below the Search box on the OPAC	Off	The link will display a listing of items that are circulated most often.
virtualshelves	OPAC	Whether to display the "Lists" button in the mast head of the OPAC	On	To create and manage lists use the Lists module in the staff client. Patrons can also create and share their reading lists.
OPACShelfBrowser	OPAC	Whether to enable the "Browse Shelf" feature in the call number column in the holdings table	Off	For this to work, you will need to have call numbers entered in field 952$o.

Configuring patron access control

In this section we'll learn how to control what patrons can and cannot do on the OPAC. These preferences control whether patrons can log on to the OPAC, change their passwords, place holds online, renew items online, write book reviews, or make purchase suggestions.

In general, most of these features are good to have and should be turned on. But if your OPAC is not available to most patrons, then it might not make sense to take on the burden of maintaining patron user IDs and passwords.

Here is a listing of these preferences along with instructions on how to set these up:

System preference	System preferences tab	Description	Default value	Instructions
opacuserlogin	OPAC	Whether to allow user login in the OPAC	On	If you turn this on, you will need to shoulder the burden of administering user names and passwords. Initial passwords will have to be distributed in a secure manner. You might get ongoing password reset requests.
OpacPasswordChange	OPAC	Whether to allow patrons to change their passwords on the OPAC	On	Set to Off if you use LDAP authentication. In this case passwords are not maintained in Koha, but on the LDAP database.
OpacRenewalAllowed	OPAC	Whether to allow renewals via the OPAC	Off	Some of the scenarios where you might want this turned off are, if you maintain hold requests outside of Koha. If you allow online renewals, the system will allow renewals even on items where there are pending hold requests.

System preference	System preferences tab	Description	Default value	Instructions
RequestOnOpac	OPAC	Whether to allow patron holds on the OPAC	On	You might want to turn this off if most of your patrons do not have access to the OPAC and you maintain hold requests outside of Koha.
reviewson	OPAC	Whether to allow patron reviews of catalog records on the OPAC	On	Reviews entered by patron will be sent for moderation by the staff. The comments can moderated in the **Comments** section under **Tools**.
suggestion	OPAC	Whether to allow purchase suggestions to be made on the OPAC	On	Patron purchase suggestions can be managed via the **Manage suggestions** section under **Acquisitions**.

Configuring enhanced content

Koha's enhanced content features help patrons select items by displaying content such as book jackets, book reviews, and ratings. This content is in addition to the regular catalog record data such as Title, Author, or Subject that is available on the OPAC, hence the term enhanced content.

Koha integrates with Web Services such as those provided by Amazon and Google to display such content. Most of these preferences are On or Off switches; others, especially Amazon-related preferences, require the appropriate keys or IDs to be set up. Some of these services are paid subscriptions; some may require login credentials to be configured.

Here is a listing of select enhanced content preferences along with instructions on how to set these up:

OPACFRBRizeEditions	System preferences tab	Description	Default value	Instructions
OPACAmazonEnabled	Enhanced Content	Whether to display Book Jackets and reviews from Amazon	Off	To get this to work, you will need to set values for the preferences **AWSAccess KeyID and AmazonAssoc Tag**. Get the key and tag from here: `http://aws.amazon.com.`
OPACAmazonCoverImages	Enhanced Content	Whether to display book jackets from Amazon	Off	To get this to work, you must turn on **OPACAmazon Enabled.** Use either Google or Amazon book jackets.
OPACAmazonSimilarItems	Enhanced Content	Whether to display Amazon's similar items feature	Off	To get this to work, you must turn on **OPACAmazon Enabled.**
GoogleJackets	Enhanced Content	Whether to display Book Jackets from Google Books	Off	Use either Google or Amazon book jackets.

OPACFRBRizeEditions	System preferences tab	Description	Default value	Instructions
OPACFRBRizeEditions	Enhanced Content	Whether to display an editions tab in the item details page	Off	To get this to work you will need one of the FRBR Web Services listed below turned on.
				Here is a definition of FRBR from Wikipedia:
		The editions tab will contain the various editions of a particular title		"Functional Requirements for Bibliographic Records — or FRBR, sometimes pronounced /'f3rber/ — is a conceptual entity-relationship model developed by the International **Federation of Library Associations and Institutions (IFLA)** that relates user tasks of retrieval and access in online library catalogues and bibliographic databases from a user's perspective. It represents a more holistic approach to retrieval and access as the relationships between the entities provide links to navigate through the hierarchy of relationships."

OPACFRBRizeEditions	System preferences tab	Description	Default value	Instructions
ThingISBN	Enhanced Content	Whether to use the **ThingISBN** web service to populate the editions tab	Off	To use this system preference you will need to first turn on **OPACFRBRize Editions**.
XISBN	Enhanced Content	Whether to use the OCLC **xISBN** Web Service to populate the editions tab	Off	To use this system preference you will need to first turn on **OPACFRBRize Editions**.
PINSEISBN	Enhanced Content	Whether to use the OINES OISBN Web Service to populate the editions tab	Off	To use this system preference you will need to first turn on **OPACFRBRize Editions**.
TagsEnabled	Enhanced Content	Whether to allow tagging of items in the OPAC	On	It is important to consider if you need tags to be moderated, see preference **TagsModeration** below.
TagsModeration	Enhanced Content	Whether tags entered by patrons need to be moderated by Library staff	Off	Tags can be moderated via the **Tags** section under **Tools**.

Configuring styling and appearance

In this section we will learn about preferences that control the styling and appearance — colors, fonts, font size, or background image of the Koha OPAC and its staff client.

Most libraries certainly want their OPAC to have a polished look, but it might be worth doing up staff client as well, as the default staff client pages are very plain.

Koha has several system preferences that control styling and appearance, with more options for the OPAC and fewer for the staff client.

These preferences related to:

- **Themes or templates**: These are a broad set of elements - style sheets, JavaScript programs, or header and footer programs – that control not just styling and appearance but also the behavior of the screens.
- **Stylesheets**: Stylesheets are CSS files, and in some cases XSLT files that relate to a narrower set of styling and appearance elements — font, color, font size, or background images.

To use these preferences effectively you will need some HTML and CSS skills.

Configuring OPAC styling and appearance

Let us look at OPAC related preferences. These preferences relate to OPAC themes, CSS style sheets, and some XSLT style sheets that control the display of MARC data.

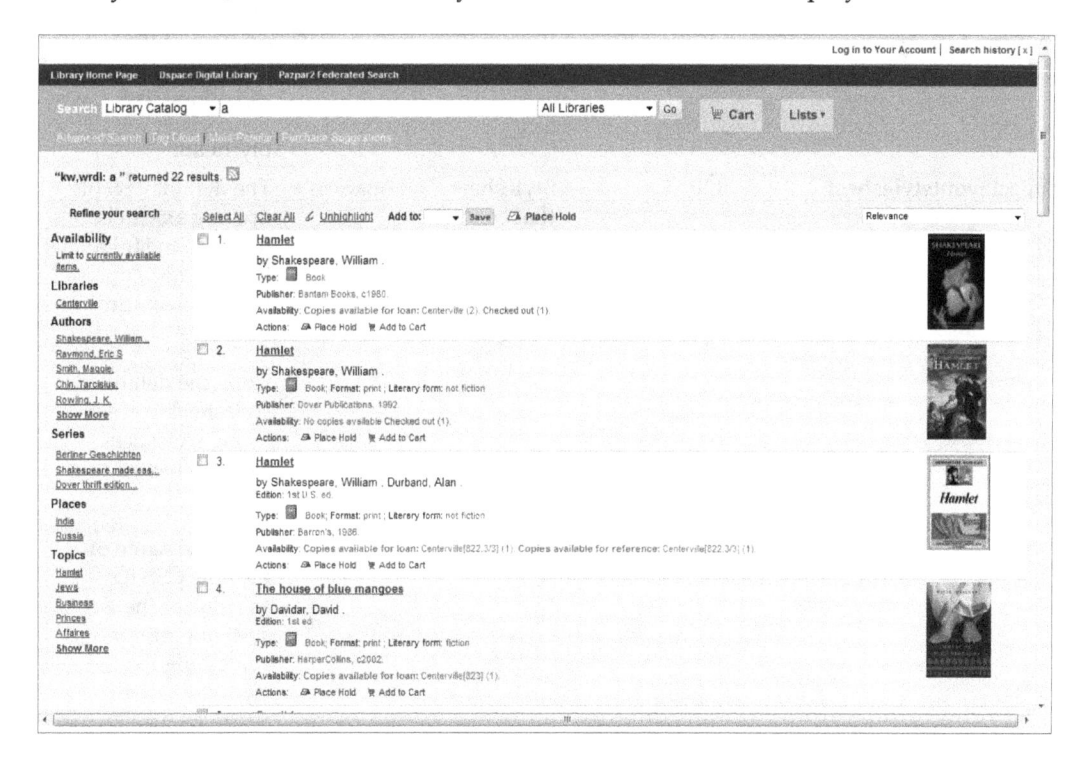

In general, to set up new themes of style sheets you will need access to the Koha server. But you also have the option of using a style sheet that is available on the web or writing CSS within the system preference.

Here is a listing of OPAC styling-related preferences along with instructions on how to set them up:

System preference	System preferences tab	Description	Default value	Instructions
opacthemes	OPAC	These themes control the style and appearance and lot of functionality	prog	The default theme "prog" is available in the folder /koha-tmpl/opac-tmpl/. You can copy the default theme folder and create a new theme. Enter the name of the new folder as value of the system preference, something like: **mytheme**
opaclayoutstylesheet	OPAC	Stylesheet that controls the layout in the OPAC	opac.css	The default CSS file opac.css can be found in the folder /koha-tmpl/opac-tmpl/prog/en/css/ Copy the default stylesheet to create a new stylesheet. Modify it as you see fit. Enter the name of the new CSS file as value of the system preference, something like: myopaclayout.css

System preference	System preferences tab	Description	Default value	Instructions
opacstylesheet	OPAC	This contains the Web URL of a stylesheet that will override the default stylesheets of Koha		This is useful if the stylesheet you want to use is maintained on a different server. Specify the full URL including the `http://`, something like: `http://mysite.com/css/mystylesheet.css`.

OPACUserCSS	OPAC	This contains the CSS code that will override default CSS settings		This is useful if you want to make minor modification to the style without having to edit the files on the server.
				
				Simply enter the code in the value box of the system preference, something like:
				
				`body {`
				`background:`
				`grey;`
				`}`

XSLTDetailsDisplay	OPAC	This preference allows us to decide whether to use XSLT stylesheets or regular CSS ones to control display of MARC record details	Off	XSLT stylesheets are a more powerful way of formatting the content. The corresponding XSLT stylesheet can be found at `/koha-tmpl/opac-tmpl/prog/en/xslt/`. The file name is: `MARC21slim2OPACDetail.xsl`.

System preference	System preferences tab	Description	Default value	Instructions
XSLTResultsDisplay	OPAC	This preference allows you to decide whether to use XSLT stylesheets or regular CSS ones to control display of record search results	Off	The XSLT stylesheet can be found at `/koha-tmpl/opac-tmpl/prog/en/xslt/`. The file name is: `MARC21slim2OPAC Results.xsl`.

Configuring staff client styling and appearance

Let us look at staff-related preferences. As with OPAC preferences, to set up new themes or templates you will need access to the Koha server, but you also have an option of pointing to an externally hosted CSS file.

These system preferences can be found under the **Staff Client** tab.

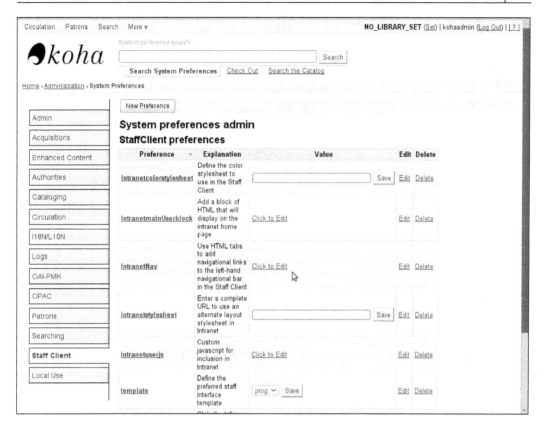

Here is a listing of preferences related to the styling of the staff client, along with instructions on how to set them up:

System preference	System preferences tab	Description	Default value	Additional information
template	Staff Client	Similar to a theme for OPAC. Templates control style, appearance, and some functionality in the staff client.	Prog	The default theme "prog" is available in the folder /koha-tmpl/ intranet-tmpl/. You can copy the default template folder and create a new template. Enter the name of the new folder as value of the system preference.

System preference	System preferences tab	Description	Default value	Additional information
intranetstylesheet	Staff Client	It contains the Web URL of a stylesheet that will override the default stylesheets of Koha.		This is useful if the stylesheet you want to use is maintained on a different server. Specify the full url including the `http://`, something like: `http://mysite.com/css/mystaffstylesheet.css`.

Configuring general preferences

And finally we turn our attention to configuring other general Koha features:

- **Messaging**: Is related to how Koha communicates with patrons
- **Security**: How access to the OPAC and the staff client is secured
- **Search**: How catalog search can be tailored to a Library's needs

Configuring messaging preferences

Libraries need to communicate with patrons for a variety of reasons—to inform them of account creation, or of upcoming events, or to remind them of overdue items.

Sometimes patrons too need to communicate with libraries, for instance to request a change in their address, or to make a purchase suggestion.

Koha can send messages to patrons via e-mail or SMS. Most Koha libraries use e-mail. We are already familiar with setting up overdue notices and trigger from previous chapters. In addition to overdue notices Koha can send other types of messages on upcoming events, when holds are fulfilled, or when items are nearly due. Libraries can choose to allow patrons to set their individual messaging preferences or the Library staff can set these up for patrons.

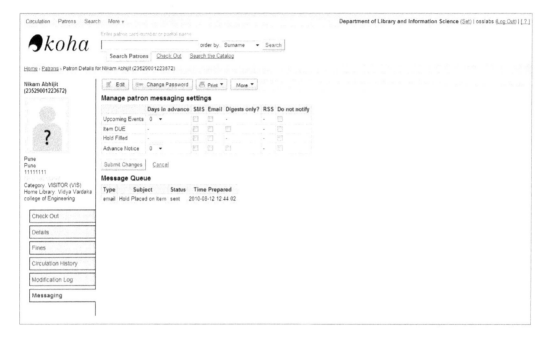

Here is a listing of messaging-related preferences along with instructions on how to set then up:

System preference	System preferences tab	Description	Default value	Additional information
EnhancedMessagingPreferences	Patrons	Whether to allow enhanced messaging preferences	Off	With this turned on, an additional **Messaging** tab becomes available in the OPAC and the staff client. Patrons or Staff can choose to receive messages on events, nearly due items, or holds that are filled.
AutoEmailOpacUser	Patrons	Whether to send an e-mail to a patron upon account creation with account details	Off	Set this to On, if you have a mail server configured and in general you have patron e-mail addresses handy when creating patron accounts.
emailLibrarianWhenHoldIsPlaced	Circulation	Whether to send an e-mail to the library e-mail address when a hold is placed	Off	Turn this On if library staff monitor e-mails more often than the Koha holds reports.

System preference	System preferences tab	Description	Default value	Additional information
AutoEmailPrimaryAddress	Patrons	The default patron email address to use when sending messages	Off	A patron record may have one or more e-mail addresses. This preference controls how the e-mail address is selected.
				Select **email** if you want the home e-mail to be used.
				Select **emailpro** if you want the office e-mail to be used.
				Select **B_email** if you want the alternate e-mail to to be used.
				Select **cardnumber** if you have e-mail addresses in the card number field.
				In above cases if the field does not have an e-mail address, notices will not be sent.
				Select "Off" if you want the first available address to be used, the system checks **email, emailpro,** and **B_email** in that order.

System preference	System preferences tab	Description	Default value	Additional information
KohaAdminEmailAddress	Admin	This address is used to both send and receive e-mails	root@ localhost	Make sure this is set to a valid e-mail address. It is also a good practice to set up e-mail addresses for each library in **Libraries, Branches and Groups** under **Administration**.

Configuring security preferences

Securing access to the OPAC and especially the staff client is important to any library. Koha's offers several ways of securing access:

- Requires valid login ID and password for both OPAC and the staff client
- Only staff users can access the staff client
- Staff access to modules with the staff client can be restricted using granular permissions
- Access to the staff client can be restricted to IP address ranges
- In multi-library installations, access to other libraries patron, circulation, and catalog data can be prevented

Most security-related preferences are under the **Admin** tab.

Here is a listing of security-related preferences with instructions on how to set them up:

System preference	System preferences tab	Description	Default value	Instructions
minPasswordLength	Patrons	The minimum length of OPAC and staff client passwords	3	The longer the minimum password length, better the security. A value of 6 is reasonable.

System preference	System preferences tab	Description	Default value	Instructions
IndependantBranches	Admin	Whether to increase security between multiple libraries or branches setup on the system	Off	Staff with super librarian privileges will not see any difference. Other staff users will not be able to view patrons of other libraries, they will not be able to edit items of other libraries nor circulate items of other libraries.
AutoLocation	Admin	Whether to block access to the staff client from unauthorized IP addresses	Off	Turn "On" to block access. Make sure you set up authorized IP addresses for each library. This can be done from **Libraries, Branches and Groups** under **Administration**.
GranularPermissions	Admin	Whether to use more detailed permissions for staff users	Off	Turn this On if you need more granular permissions when setting permissions for staff users. More granularity becomes available for tools, circulation, and serials modules.
timeout	Admin	Duration after which a user's session should time out	12000000	This is in seconds. Reduce this value to decrease the risk of someone misusing another staff member's idle session.

Configuring search preferences

The catalog search tool is available on both the OPAC and the staff client. It is the most frequently used tool. Although the default search-related system preference should work for most libraries, it might be a good idea to consider changing some of these preferences to better tailor the search to your library's needs.

The search related system preferences can found under the **Searching** tab.

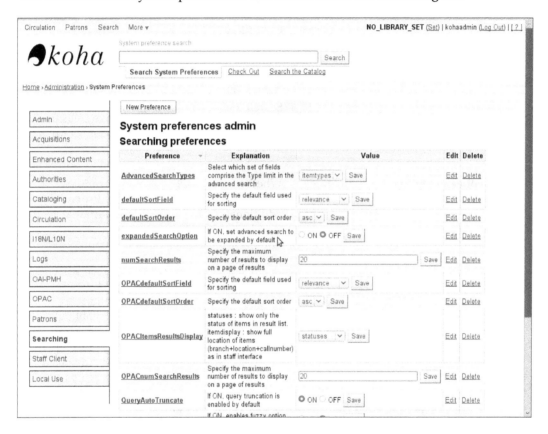

Here is the explanation of the search-related preferences along with instructions on configuring them:

System preference	System preferences tab	Description	Default value	Instructions
AdvancedSearchTypes	Searching	Whether to use Item types or Collection codes as search limits in the Advanced Search tool	itemtypes	Search limits allow one to search within item types or collection codes. To use collection codes, your records must have collection codes set up in the collection code field 952$8.
expandedSearchOption	Searching	Whether to display additional search options in the advanced search page by default or only when "more options" are clicked.	Off	Turn "On" to display additional options by default. To see what additional options are available, click on the **More Options** link in the **Advanced Search** page on the OPAC.
QueryRemoveStopwords	Searching	Whether to remove stop words from search query strings	Off	If turned on, the system will automatically remove from search strings words that are set up in **Stop Words** under **Koha Administration**.

Summary

Here is what we learned in this chapter:

- How to browse system preferences categories or to find them using the search tool
- Configuring Patrons, Acquisitions, and Serials preferences
- Configuring OPAC preferences—static content, tools for patrons, patron access control, and enhanced content
- Configuring styling and appearance on the OPAC and the staff client
- Configuring messaging, security, and search related preferences

This completes our application configuration work and we ready to use Koha. In the next chapter, we will conduct a test drive of our newly installed and configured Koha installation.

8
Test Driving Your Koha Installation

We have completed the server setup and the application configuration. We are now in a position to take our Koha installation for a test drive. We will look to complete a transaction cycle in each of the primary Koha modules:

- Patrons
- Cataloging
- Circulation
- Acquisition
- Serials

We will also test:

- The reports module
- The catalog search on the OPAC

Patrons—create, search, and view patron record

Let us first create a patron record. A patron record includes the patron's personal details such as name, date of birth, or address. Staff also need to specify the library the patron belongs to and his/her patron category. A user ID and password for use on the OPAC can also be set up.

Creating a new patron

To create a patron record, navigate to the **Patrons** module using the menu bar at the top of the page and click on the **New** button in the **Patrons** home page. You will need to select the appropriate **Patron Category** first.

While you are creating the patron, you should verify the correctness of the following system preferences and administrative settings related to:

- Borrower's mandatory fields
- Membership expiry date calculation
- Auto card number generation
- Minimum password length

Searching for a patron

Let us make sure the patron has been saved successfully. Use the **Search Patrons** tab under the search box to search for the particular patron.

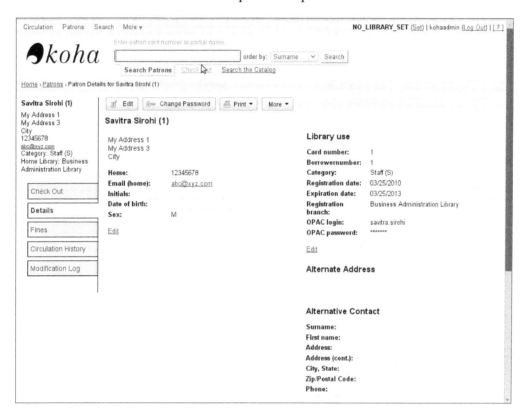

Cataloging—create, search, and view bibliographic and item record

In this section let us create a complete catalog record—a bibliographic record first, and then an item record under it.

Creating a bibliographic record

To create a new record, navigate to the **Cataloging** module using the **More** drop-down list in the menu bar on the top of the page. Then use the **New Record** button. You will need to select the appropriate MARC framework first.

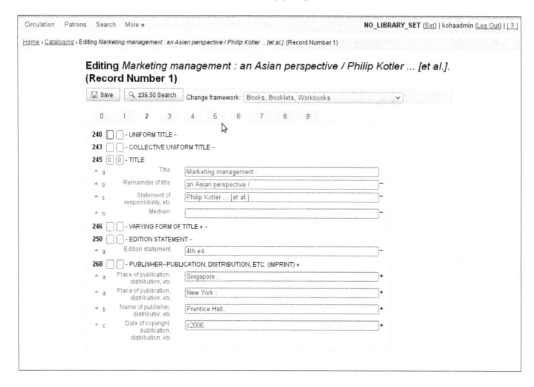

You can use the Z39.50 search feature to find and import records from the Library of Congress and other Z39.50 servers.

While you are cataloging the record, you might want to cross check your MARC framework settings:

- Fields displayed
- Mandatory fields
- Fields under Authority Control
- Fields under Authorized Values control

Creating an item record

Once the bibliographic record is created, you will automatically move to the **Add Item** screen.

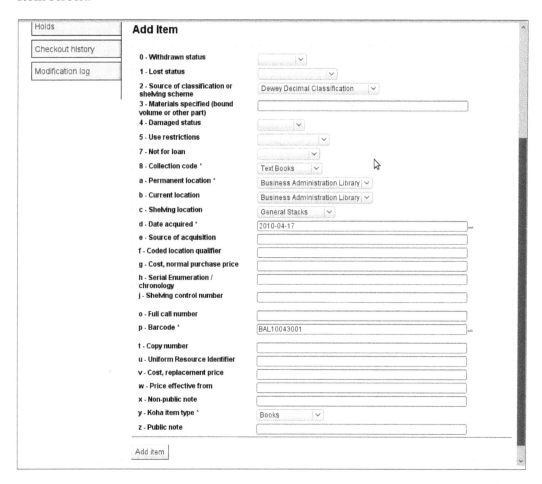

While adding the item record, you might want to cross check your MARC framework settings:

- Fields displayed
- Mandatory fields
- Fields under Authority Control
- Fields under Authorized Values control

Searching for the record

Let us now make sure the bibliographic and item records are saved properly. Use the **Search the Catalog** tab under the search box to search for the record you just added.

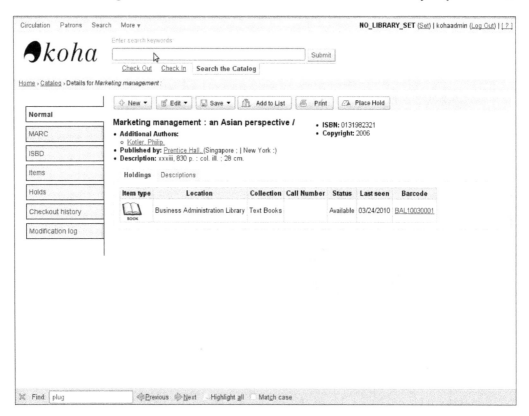

Circulation—check-out, check-in, and view circulation history

Now that we have a catalog record and a patron record, we are in a position to test circulation. We will perform a check-out operation followed by a check-in operation.

Checking out

First navigate to the **Circulation** module using the menu bar on the top of the page. Then enter the name of the patron or the patron's card number in the search box. Make sure you are using the **Check Out** tab under the search box.

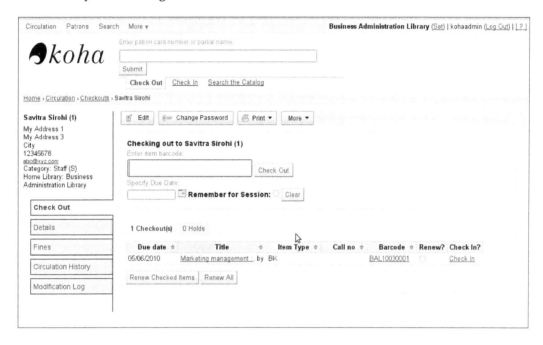

Once you click on **Submit**, you will enter the barcode of the item to be checked out.

During the operation you should verify that the due date is calculated in accordance with system preferences or administrative settings related to:

- Calculation of due date
- Holidays setup in the calendar

Checking in

To check in, use the **Check In** tab under the search box. You will need to enter the item's barcode.

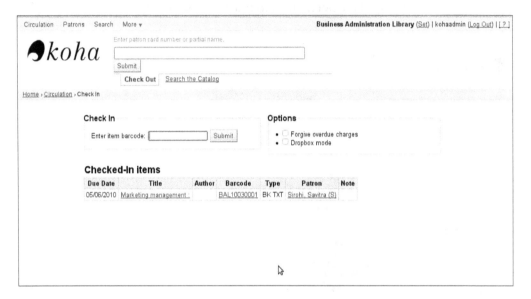

Viewing circulation history

Let us verify if the check-out and check-in operations were successful. Find the patron using the **Search Patrons** feature. Then click on the **Circulation History** tab to find the check out and check in records.

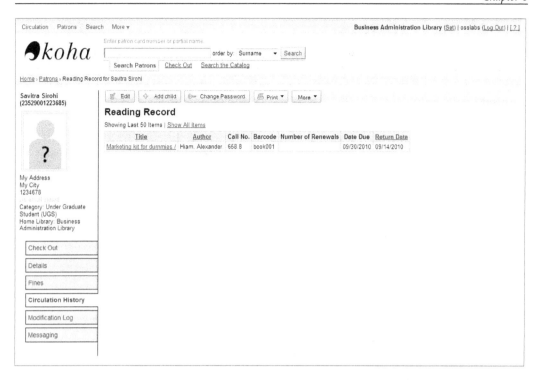

Acquisitions—create an order, receive shipment, and view budget utilization

To test the Acquisitions module we will create a budget, a vendor, and an order basket. We will then receive the shipment and finally test the impact of the order on the budget availability figures.

Creating budgets

Navigate to the **Funds and budgets** section under Koha **Administration**. First create a **Fund** by entering a code, a name and optionally, indicate to the library what the fund is for. Then click on the **Add Budget** link. Enter the **Fund** and the **Budget amount**. Optionally, enter in the **Library** what the budget is for and the **Start date** and **End date**.

Creating a vendor

Before we create an order basket, we need to create a vendor — a book seller or a publisher. Navigate to the **Acquisitions** module using the **More** drop-down list. Then click on the **New Vendor** button to enter the vendor details.

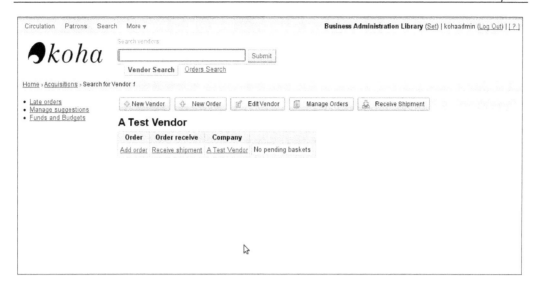

Creating orders

To create an order basket click on the **New Order** button on the **Add order** link. Once you enter the order details you should see an order basket summary. You can modify the basket at this stage. Once the order is finalized, click on the **Close this basket** link.

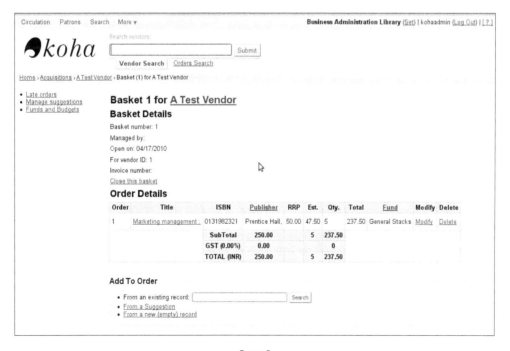

Receiving shipments

To receive a shipment, click on the **Receive Shipment** button.

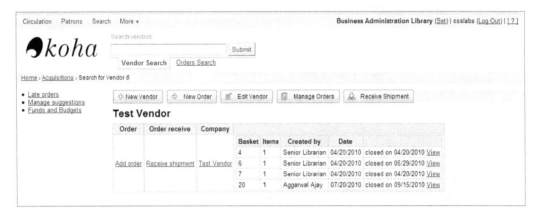

You will need to enter barcode and other details for each item in the shipment. Use the [+] link above the **Save** button to create a new empty block for each copy. Once you accession each copy, click on **Save** to finish the process of receiving items.

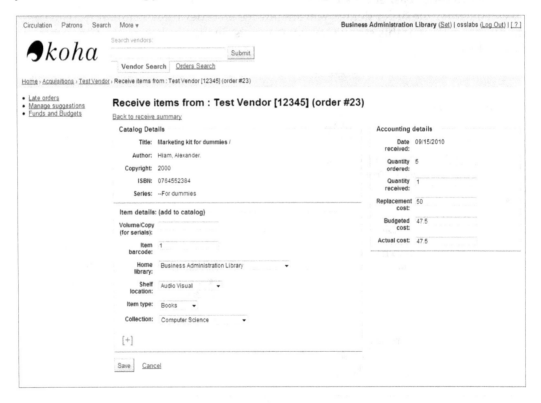

Viewing budget utilization

Finally, let us take a peek at the budget figures; the **Spent** and **Avail** amount will be automatically changed to reflect the order you just closed.

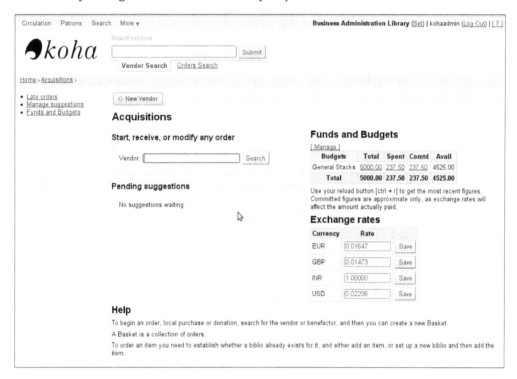

Serials—creating a subscription and receiving the first issue

Let us now test the Serials module. This module is used to manage serials or periodicals. Staff enter information about the subscription such as the vendor, the related bibliographic record, the frequency of receiving issue or numbering pattern, and subscription length. The subscription record is then used to track receipt of issues and the renewal of the subscription.

We will first create subscription and then receive the first issue for this subscription.

Creating a subscription

Navigate to the **Serials** module using the **More** drop-down list. Click on the **New Subscription** button to enter the subscription details.

Fields with labels in red are mandatory.

Here are the steps to entering subscription details:

1. Select a vendor by using the **Search for a vendor** link
2. Use the **Search for Biblio** or the **Create Biblio** links to link a bibliographic record to the subscription
3. Choose whether you want an item record for each issue or not
4. Enter other details such as **Call Number** and **Library** the subscription belongs to

Here are steps to Serials planning:

1. Enter the **First issue publication date**, this is the publication date of the first issue that will arrive in the library
2. Enter the **Frequency**; there are several options available such as **1/month** or **1/week**
3. Choose the **Numbering pattern** of the Serial
4. Enter the **Starting with** and **Rollover at** details
5. Use the **Test Prediction Pattern** button to test whether the pattern is correct. You should see a message **No irregularities noticed**.
6. Click on the **Save Subscription** button

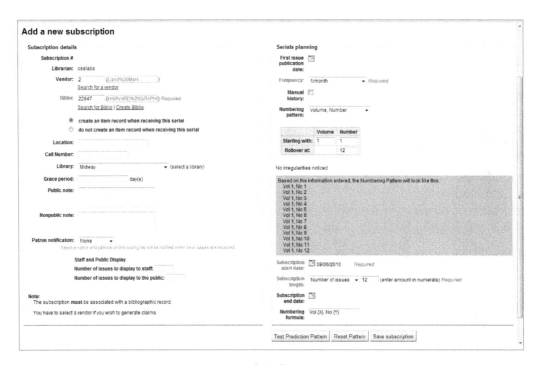

Searching for the subscription

Let us make sure that the subscription is saved successfully. Use the **Search Subscriptions** tab to find the record. Enter either the **ISSN** or the **Title** of the subscription and click on the **Search** button.

Receiving an issue

When the issue arrives in the Library, the staff needs to update the subscription record to account for this event. To receive an issue, we use the **Receive** button as shown in the previous screenshot.

Reports—creating a guided report and executing it

Let us now test the Reports module. This module allows staff to create reports using a guided reports wizard or using SQL statements. Reports that are created can be saved and generated at a later time. This module also has statistics wizards for various functional modules and a few commonly used pre-built reports.

In this test drive we create a guided report and test its execution.

Building a report

Navigate to the **Reports** home page using the **More** drop-down list. Click on the **Guided Reports** link. Use the **Build New** button to launch the guided reports wizard.

We go through the following steps to create the report:

1. Select the module that we want to query.

2. Choose the display format.

3. Choose a set of fields for the reports' columns.

4. Set selection criteria or limits.

5. Configure how you want data to be totaled.

6. Choose how you want the report to be ordered.

Click on the **Finish** button to create the report. You will need to save the report before using it.

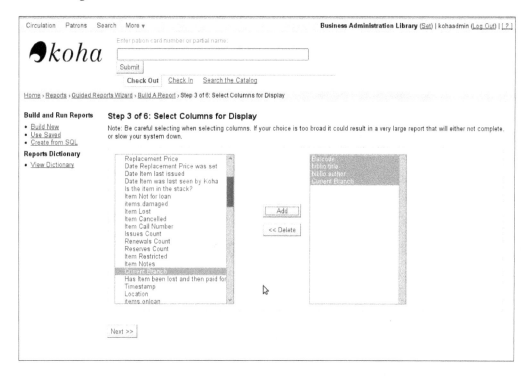

Using a saved report

To test the report you just created click on the **Use Saved** button on link. Click on the **Run this Report** link to execute the report. You also have an option of downloading the report in a comma separated format. The file can then be opened in a spreadsheet program for further analysis.

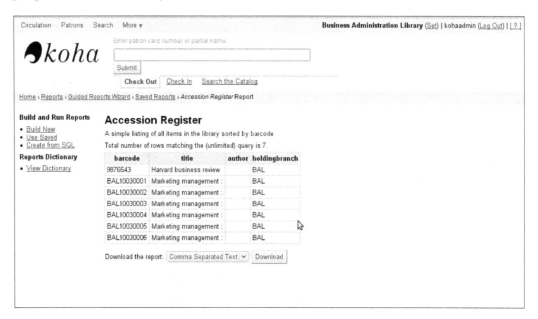

OPAC—running a catalog search

And finally let us test the catalog search feature on the OPAC. Simply type in a word or phrase related to record(s) you know are in the catalog and click on the **Go** button. You should see results sorted by **Relevance** and the **Refine your search** block on the left populated with Libraries, Authors, and Topics related to the search results. This test tells us that our Zebra setup is functioning well.

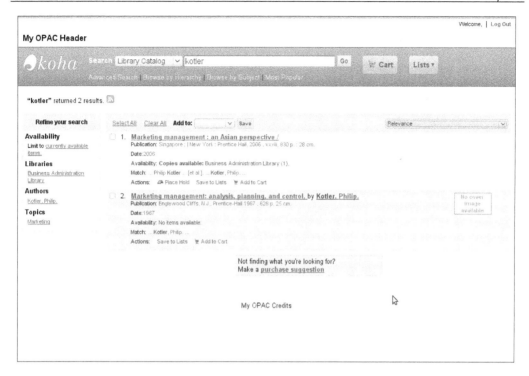

Summary

In this chapter we tested the primary Koha modules to ensure that the software installation and the server and application configuration were performed correctly.

We ran test cycles as follows:

- Patrons—create, search, and view a patron record
- Cataloging—create, search, and view a bibliographic and item record
- Circulation—check out, check in an item, and view its circulation history
- Acquisition—create an order basket, receive shipment, and view updated budget utilization
- Serials—create a subscription and receive the first issue
- Reports—create a guided report and execute it
- OPAC—executed a catalog search

In the next chapter, we will learn how to import catalog data into our Koha installation.

9
Migrating Catalog Data

Migrating catalog data from the legacy system is a prerequisite to using Koha for most libraries. The process involves exporting MARC records from the legacy system and importing them into Koha using Koha's import tools.

Migrating bibliographic data is usually easy; holdings data, however, presents a few challenges. This stems from the fact that different library systems record holdings data in different ways—fields and subfields used for an element may be different. In some cases, certain fields used in Koha may not be directly available in the holdings field.

In this chapter we will learn how to convert MARC files from legacy systems into Koha compatible files. We will learn about Koha's MARC record import tools.

An orientation to migrating catalog data

Let's start by getting a better understanding of the migration process. Here is what we will cover in this orientation section:

- The structure of MARC files that we will import into Koha
- How Koha's holdings MARC field differs from the corresponding field in other systems
- The tools we will employ to convert and import the catalog data into Koha

Understanding MARC files

We will need to convert MARC files exported from the legacy system, which have an extension .mrc. Let's understand more about the structure of such files:

- Records: Each MARC file will contain one or more MARC records. Each MARC record contains bibliographic data and one or more holdings fields.

- Bibliographic data: Each MARC record contains bibliographic data, such as title, author, ISBN, or subject.

- Holdings fields: Information on the physical copies—such as library, barcode number, shelving location, or collection code, is recorded in a holdings field. A catalog record may have multiple holdings fields, one for each copy that is available in the library.

Koha Holdings in tag 952

Koha keeps holdings data in tag 952. We will need to make sure that the records in the import file have the data mapped to the 952 tag and to the corresponding subfields under this tag.

You can view Koha's subfields under tag 952 in the **MARC Bibliographic framework** section under **Koha Administration**.

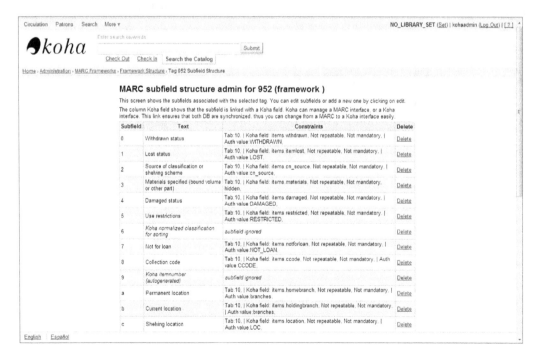

Some 952 subfields are very important from a Koha perspective. These include:

- 952$a — Permanent location: This is the home library or branch of the particular item. It is important for circulation purposes that this subfield should have a valid library code.

- 952$b — Current location: Usually the same as home library or branch; this too must have a valid library code.

- 952$y — Koha item type: Item types are used for setting up circulation rules. This field must have a valid item-type code.

- 952$p — Piece designation: This is the item barcode. Circulation would not be possible without data in this subfield.

Holdings in legacy systems

It is likely that you will see these differences between Koha's holdings field and the holdings field on records exported from the legacy system:

- The holdings tag is likely to be 852, rather than tag 952.

- Holdings subfields will differ from what Koha uses. The subfields may fully or partially comply with the Library of Congress MARC 21 holdings standards available here: http://www.loc.gov/marc/holdings/hd852.html.

- Some of the important Koha subfields may not be available — Permanent location and Current location, or Koha item type.

- Koha stores the item call number in a single subfield 952$o, but in the legacy MARC record, you will likely find the call number broken into multiple subfields — $h: Classification part, $i: Item part, and $k: Call number prefix.

Import tools

To import the data into Koha, we first convert the source MARC File into a Koha-compatible file using MARCEdit — a free MARC editor.

We then import the converted file using one of Koha's imports tools:

- `bulkmarcimport.pl`: A Linux command-line tool usually used to import large MARC files

- GUI import tool: A more flexible import tool available in Koha's staff client

Here is more information about these tools:

MARCEdit

A very popular tool used to view and edit MARC records, and convert them from text to MARC and vice versa. The software is free to download and use, but runs only on Windows.

MARCEdit is available for download at this link: `http://people.oregonstate.edu/~reeset/marcedit/html/downloads.html`.

For the purposes of migrating catalog data, we will use MARCEdit to manipulate the source file to make it suitable for importing into Koha; we will:

- Replace holdings field and subfields with ones used in Koha
- Add holdings subfields that are missing in the source MARC file
- Merge Call number-related subfields into Koha's single Call number subfield

bulkmarckimport.pl

This is a Koha program that can import MARC records from a file; it is usually used for importing files with a very large number of records. We run this program from the Linux terminal.

The program is available in the folder `/misc/migration_tools`. To learn about this program, try running it with the `-h` option:

```
linux-4yut:/usr/share/kohaclone/misc/migration_tools # ./bulkmarcimport.
pl --h
Small script to import bibliographic records into Koha.
```

Bulkmarcimport.pl option	Mandatory?	Explanation	Example
`file`	Yes	This is the full path to the MARC file that you wish to import. You will always need to use this option.	`-file /home/koha/importfile.mrc`
`v`	No	Output more information, optionally add a "1" or "2" for additional information.	`-v` or `-v 1` or `-v 2`

Bulkmarcimport.pl option	Mandatory?	Explanation	Example
fk	No	When importing records, values for fields such as library code (952$a) need to be present in the Koha database. Use this option to turn off such checks during imports; records will be imported even if the corresponding data is not present in the database.	-fk
n	No	The number of records to import from a file, if not used all the records are imported.	-n 1000
o	No	The number of records from the start of the file that are to be skipped.	-o 1000
commit	No	The number of records that are committed in a batch. 50 records per commit is the default. If your import is too slow, you might consider increasing this value; however, remember that if the program crashes due to a certain record, all the other records in the batch will be lost as well.	-commit 100
t	No	It is useful to run a new import file in the test mode initially. The program does minimal processing and may warn you of potential problems. However, remember that a successful test does not mean there will be no problem with the actual import.	-t
s	No	Koha automatically converts any MARC-8 records to UTF-8. If you see a problem with the format of imported data in Koha screens, you may want to try this option to see if it yields better results.	-s

Bulkmarcimport.pl option	Mandatory?	Explanation	Example
c	No	The characteristic MARC flavor of records in the import file. Default is MARC21.	-c UNIMARC
d	No	Deletes all catalog records in the database prior to importing the file. Be very careful with this option, there is no way to recover lost records.	-d
m	No	The format of the records in the import file. Default is ISO2709, if you are importing XML, use the MARCXML option.	-m MARCXML
x	No	The tag containing a record identifier, this refers to a tag in the records in the import file.	-x 020
y	No	The subfield containing the record identifier, this subfield is for the tag identified by option x above. Option y cannot be used with option x.	-y a
idmap	No	Path and name of a file containing a map between the record identifier and the biblionumber that is generated when the record is inserted into Koha. The record identfier is contained in the field specified by options x and y above. The file is generated by bulkmarcimport.pl when it is executed. The file can be useful for troubleshooting the migration process or for maintaining a record of how the records were migrated.	-idmap /home/ idmapfilename

IMPORTANT: Don't use this script before you've entered and checked your MARC parameters tables twice (or more!). Otherwise, the import won't work correctly and you will get invalid data.

```
SAMPLE:
  $ export KOHA_CONF=/etc/koha.conf
  $ perl misc/migration_tools/bulkmarcimport.pl -d -commit 1000 \
    -file /home/jmf/koha.mrc -n 3000
```

Koha's GUI import tool

Koha also is an end-user-friendly GUI import tool. The catalog import is executed in two steps:

- **Stage MARC Records for Import**: Here we load the records into a reservoir
- **Manage Staged MARC records**: Here we review and complete the import

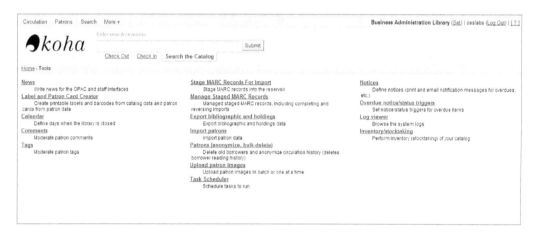

This tool is more sophisticated when compared to `bulkmarcimport.pl`, as it allows for:

- Review of records prior to import
- An undo import operation
- Support for record matching rules

Record matching rules can match the incoming records to those already in the database. These rules can be used to:

- Add holdings to existing bibliographic records
- Replace bibliographic records with new ones

Choosing an import tool

Here are some pointers to help you decide which tool to employ when importing MARC files:

- In general, `bulkmarcimport.pl` is better when you are setting up Koha for the first time. It is faster and can handle large files.
- If you need to import new records into an existing Koha database, say when migrating data from a new branch, it is better to use the GUI tool. We can use matching rules to ensure that holdings are attached to a single parent bibliographic record.

Migration process

The process is as follows:

- Use MARCEdit to manipulate the source MARC file and make it suitable for import into Koha
- We will need to setup values in administrative fields in Koha corresponding to data in fields, such as library, item type, collection, or shelving location in the source MARC file
- Use either the `bulkmarcimport.pl` or the GUI import tools to import the MARC file

Preparing to migrate catalog data

Now that we have an understanding of the migration process, let's learn how to prepare for the migration. We prepare the plan in two parts; first, we determine how we will source data for the holdings subfields in Koha. Next, we decide what data we will need to setup in Koha prior to importing the MARC file.

Mapping Koha's holdings subfields to subfields in source MARC file

In the first part of the plan, we set up a table listing all of Koha's holdings subfields. We map each subfield to a corresponding subfield in the source file. If corresponding fields for any mandatory Koha fields are not available in the source file, we will need to add data manually for such subfields while editing the file.

Koha field	Mandatory	Corresponding field in ource MARC file	Comments
952$8: Collection code	No	852$b	
952$a: Permanent location	Yes	Not available in source file	MARC file has been exported by Library. We will manually add this tag to all records in the file.
952$b: Current location	Yes	Not available in source file	Same as Permanent location.
952$c: Shelving location		Not available in source file	
952$d: Date acquired		852$c	
952$e: Source of acquisition		852$x	
952$g: Cost, purchase price		852$9	
952$o: Full call number		852$h and 852$i	
952$p: Piece designation	Yes	852$p	
952$t: Copy number		Not available in source file	
952$v: Cost, replacement price		Not available in source file	
952$x: Non-public note		Not available in source file	
952$y: Koha's item type	Yes	Not available in source file	MARC file has been exported by item type. We will manually add this tag to all records in the file.
952$z: Public note		Not available in source file	

Planning setup of administrative fields in Koha

In the second part of the plan, we plan how to setup values in Koha's administrative fields. We need to ensure that libraries, item types, collection codes, and shelving locations in the various MARC records in the source files are setup in Koha prior to importing the file. We prepare a plan as follows:

Field in source MARC file	Distinct values in source MARC file	Koha's administrative fields where the values need to be setup
Library or Branch code	Lib1	Libraries in **Libraries and Groups** under **Koha Administration.**
Item Type	BOOK	Koha's **Item types** under **Koha Administration.**
	CD	
	DVD	
	JR	
	REF	
Collection Code	Biography	**Authorized values** under **Koha Administration**. Setup under category – **CCODE.**
	Business	
	Fiction	
	General	
	History	
	Humour	
Shelving Location	AV	**Authorized values** under **Koha Administration**. Setup under category – **LOC.**
	Dis	
	New	
	Ref	

Migrating catalog data

In this section, we demonstrate how to implement our migration plan. We edit the source file using MARCEdit, setup administrative fields in Koha, and then use either the `bulkmarcimport.pl` or the GUI import tool to complete the migration.

Setting up values in Koha's administrative fields

First, we need to make sure that we prepare the Koha database for importing the new records by setting values in administrative fields, such as library, item type, or collection code.

Setting up branch codes

The branch code(s) can be setup from **Libraries and Groups** page under **Koha Administration**.

Setting up Item types

The Item type(s) can be setup from the **Item Types** page under **Koha Administration**.

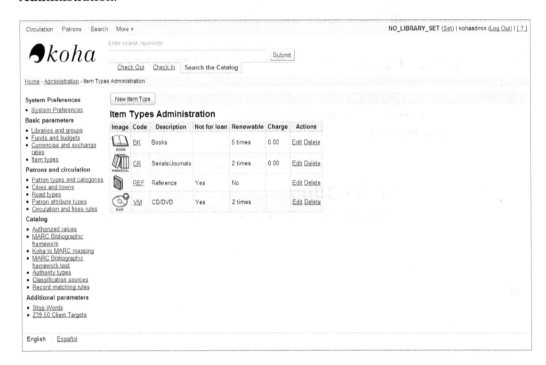

Setting up collection codes

The collection code(s) can be setup from the **Authorized values** page under **Koha Administration**. Add values to the category **CCODE**.

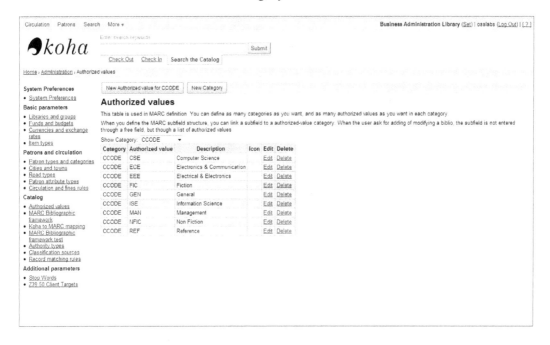

Setting up shelving locations

The item type(s) can be setup from the **Authorized values** page under **Koha Administration**. Add values to the category **LOC**.

Editing the source MARC file using MARCEdit

To edit the import file, we use MARCEdit.

Use the **MarcBreaker** tool to convert the MARC file into a readable file with the extension `.mrk`.

Click on the **Edit Records** button to view the records.

Use the various options under MARCEdit's **Edit** and **Tools** menu to create the file as per Koha's standards. Here are instructions on some of the key operations you are likely to need—swapping subfields, adding a new subfield, and merging subfields:

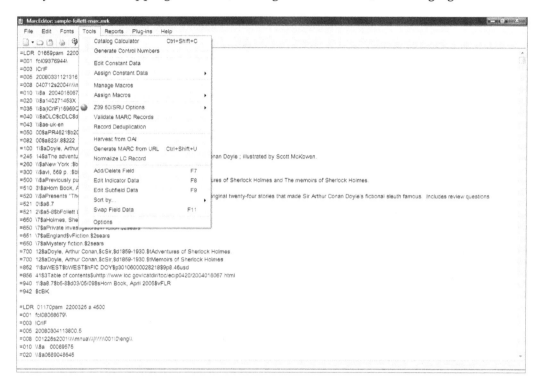

Swapping subfields

To swap fields, use the **Swap Field Data** tool under the **Tools** menu. Here are the steps to swapping subfields:

1. Specify **Field** and **Subfield** for the **Original** and **Modified** data.

2. Check **Copy Source** if you want to retain the original holdings field.

3. Check **Add to existing field**; this way you ensure that newly swapped subfields are included in the same holdings tag.

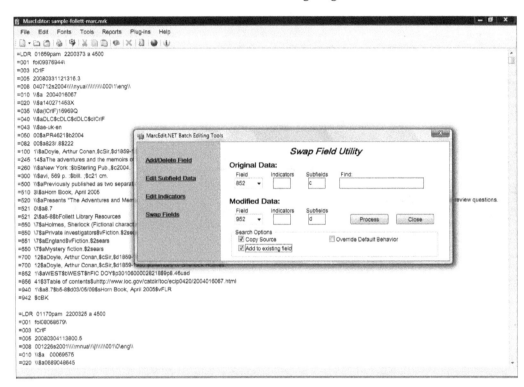

Adding a new subfield

To add a new field, use the **Add/Delete Field** utility under the **Tools** menu. Enter **Field** as 952, and **Field data** as `\\<subfield><value>`. For instance, to add a 952$a with value LIB1, enter **Field data** as `\\$aLIB1`.

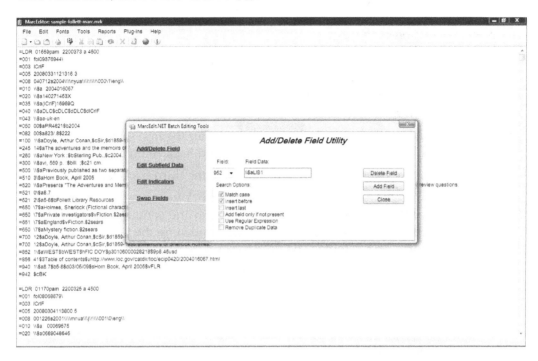

Merging subfields

To merge call number fields in the source file into a single a single call number field in Koha—952$o, we need to use regular expressions. Here are the steps:

1. Swap each subfield in source holdings field to corresponding subfields under 952

2. Setup a regular expression find and replace that merges a set of subfields

Setting up a regular expression can be tricky, and readers are encouraged to get introduced to regular expressions first. Here is a handy introductory tutorial:

`http://www.regular-expressions.info/tutorial.html`

Let's now look at a specific example—merging subfields $h and $i, with a space between the two values, into Koha's call number subfield $o.

First, we setup a **Find** expression as follows:

(=952 \\\\)(.*)(\\$h)([a-zA-Z0-9.]*)(.*)(\\$i)([a-zA-Z0-9.]*)(.*)

Here is an explanation of this expression:

- **(=952 \\\\)**: Look for the pattern =952 \\. We have four \ in the expression instead of two, because \ is a special character, and we need to escape each occurrence with another \. The round brackets store the matched string in the first back-reference field.
- **(.*)**: Look for any string including "nothing" after the first search pattern, and stores whatever is matched into the second back-reference field.
- **(\\$h)**: Look for the subfield $h, and store it in the third back-reference field. $ is a special character too and is escaped using a \.
- **([a-zA-Z0-9.]*)**: Look for a string that follows $h and contains any number of small letters, capital letters, numbers, or ., and store the matched string into the fourth back reference field.
- **(.*)**: Match any string including "nothing" after the $h subfield, and store it in the fifth back-reference field.
- **(\\$i)**: Look for the subfield $i, and store it in the sixth back-reference field.
- **([a-zA-Z0-9.]*)**: Look for a string that follows $i and contains any number of small letters, capital letters, numbers, or ., and store the matched string into the seventh back-reference field.
- **(.*)**: Match any string after the $i subfield, and store it into the eighth back-reference field.

And then, we setup the **Replace** expression as follows:

1o$4 $7$2$5$8

Here is an explanation of the **Replace** expression:

- **$1:** In the replace string start with the value in the first back-reference field, the value here is =952 \\
- **$o**: Append the subfield label $o
- **$4:** Append the value of the subfield $h that is stored in the fourth back-reference field
- **<space>**: Append a space as a separator
- **$7:** Append the value of the subfield $i that is stored in the seventh back-reference field
- **$2:** Append the text if any, before the $h subfield; this is stored in the second back-reference field
- **$5:** Append the text, if any between the $h and $i subfields, this is stored in the fifth back-reference field
- **$8:** Append the text after the $i subfield, this is stored in the eighth back-reference field

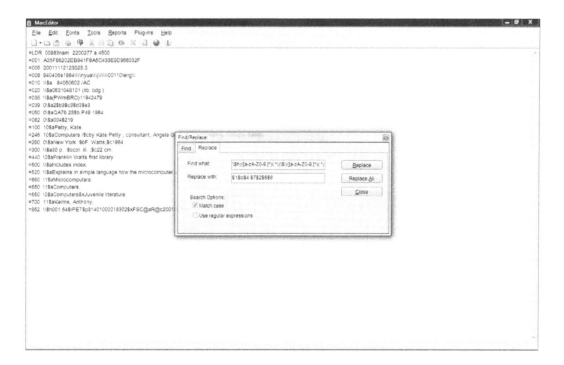

Once you are done, use the **Compile File into MARC** option under the **File** menu to create your new MARC file.

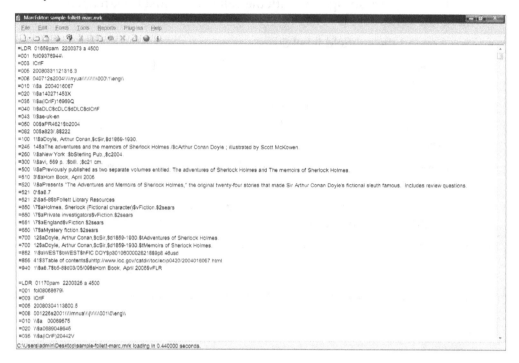

Importing the MARC file

The `bulkmarcimport.pl` program is the preferred way to import a large number of records. It is usually used during the initial phases of migration to Koha.

Using the bulkmarcimport.pl program

Before we run the program, let's make sure the shell environment variables are set correctly:

```
linux-4yut:/usr/share/kohaclone/misc/migration_tools # echo $PERL5LIB
/usr/share/kohaclone
linux-4yut:/usr/share/kohaclone/misc/migration_tools # echo $KOHA_CONF
/etc/koha-dev/etc/koha-conf.xml
```

That looks ok. If you see empty variables, you can set them using these commands:

```
linux-4yut:/usr/share/kohaclone/misc/migration_tools # export PERL5LIB=/
usr/share/kohaclone
```

```
linux-4yut:/usr/share/kohaclone/misc/migration_tools # export KOHA_CONF=/
etc/koha-dev/etc/koha-conf.xml
```

To import a file, we run the command as follows:

```
linux-4yut:/usr/share/kohaclone/misc/migration_tools # ./bulkmarcimport.
pl -d -file /home/koha/Download/sample-marc
deleting biblios
300............................................................................
............................
322 MARC records done in 15.4088408946991 seconds
```

Note the use of -d option; this deletes all the data in the catalog before importing the file.

Importing catalog records using the GUI tools

You can use Koha's GUI tool to import the MARC file. Here are the steps to staging the records and managing staged records:

Staging MARC records for import

The first stage of the import process is to stage the records. Koha will import the records into a temporary storage area without changing the actual bibliographic or holdings data.

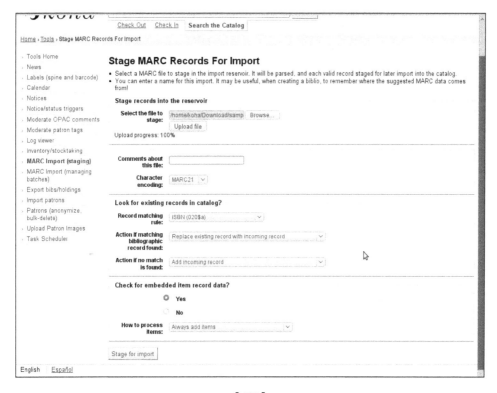

Koha comes preconfigured with two matching rules, one that matches on ISBN, and the other on ISSN. By using matching rules, you can make sure that all items or copies are grouped under the same parent bibliographic record.

Here are the steps to staging your MARC file:

1. Select the MARC file, and click on **Upload** to load the MARC file.

2. Select the matching rule (**ISBN** for books and ISSN for serials).

3. Set **Action if matching bibliographic records found** to **ignore**.

4. Set **Action if no match is found** to **Add incoming record**.

5. Say **Yes** to **Check for embedded item record data**.

6. Set **How to process items** to **Always add items**.

At the end of the process, Koha will let you review the records before you actually import the records.

Managing records

In this step, the records will be imported into Koha's database. Simply click on the **Import into Catalog** button to start the process.

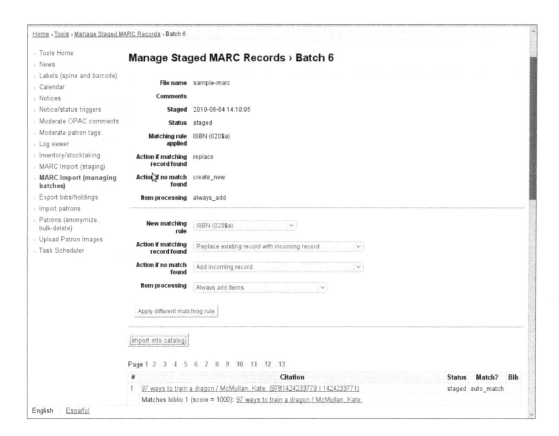

Once the import completes, you will see a summary of the import.

Undo Import

The great thing about the GUI tool is that it is possible to undo an import. Simply click on the **Undo import into catalog** button.

Summary

Here is what we learned in this chapter on migrating catalog data from MARC compliant legacy library systems:

- Using MARCEdit to manipulate source MARC files
- Adding, merging, or swapping holdings subfields
- Setting up administrative fields in Koha prior to importing MARC files
- Using `bulkmarcimport.pl` and the GUI import tools

This completes the implementation section of this book. In the next chapter, we will learn how to troubleshoot installation and migration problems.

10
Troubleshooting

In this chapter, we will look at ways to troubleshoot problems with our Koha installation. If you are responsible for ensuring the availability of your Koha installation, troubleshooting is a key skill that you will need to develop. You may face problems during installation, during upgrades, or when users use the system in new ways.

We will first look at the community tools and resources available to you for help:

- Koha's Mailing lists
- Koha's IRC chat
- Koha's bug tracker
- Koha's Git repository

We will also look at ways to troubleshoot and fix some common problems:

- Apache2 web server is down
- MySQL database server is down
- Zebra search is not returning any results
- Zebra index rebuild is not working
- Parser problems
- Over dues e-mails not working
- Fines not working
- Software bugs
- Command-line programs — environment variables not exported
- Problems with Internet Explorer

Where to get help—community resources

There are several tools and resources that you can use to get help from the Koha community. In this section, we will point to you these resources.

Koha's mailing lists

You should join the main Koha list; this is the users list, it is very active, and is the best way to get support from the community. You can consider joining other specialized lists, depending on your interest.

You can join the lists via this page:

`http://koha-community.org/support/koha-mailing-lists/.`

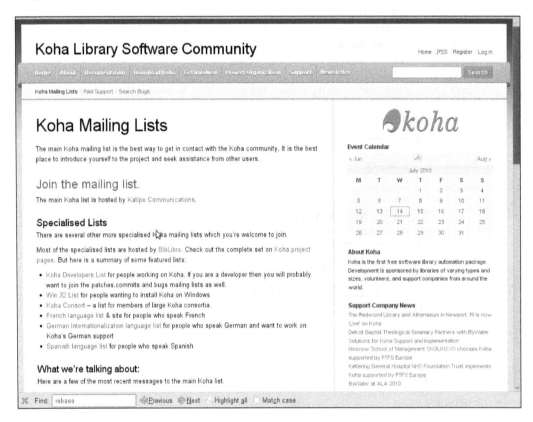

Koha's IRC chat

If you need to chat with Koha developers in real time, you should use the IRC chat. You can join the chat via this page:

`http://koha-community.org/support/.`

 The IRC server is `irc.katipo.co.nz` and channel is `#koha`.

Koha's bug tracker

Koha's bug tracker is available at this URL:

`http://bugs.koha-community.org/bugzilla3/.`

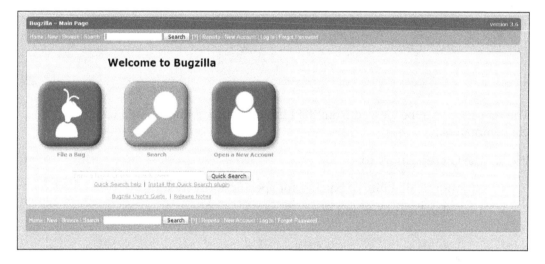

We use the bug tracker to:

- File a new bug report
- View a bug's status
- Learn about any work-around to the problem
- Download patches that fix the problem, especially if the fix is not available in Koha's Git repository

Koha's Git repository

A web display of Koha's Git software repository is available at at:

```
http://git.koha-community.org/.
```

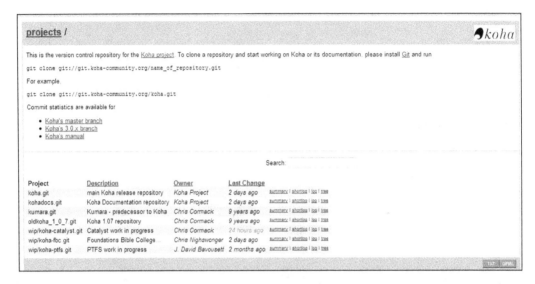

The repository can be viewed from the Linux command line, as well using Git commands.

We use the Git repository to:

- Monitor availability of patches for specific software bugs
- Download software updates

Common problems

In this section, we will look at ways to troubleshoot some common problems with a Koha installation. Other than software bugs, most other problems stem from improper server or application configuration. For each problem, we demonstrate diagnosis and rectification steps.

Apache2 web server is down

If the Apache2 web server is down, you will not be able to connect to the server; you should see something like this.

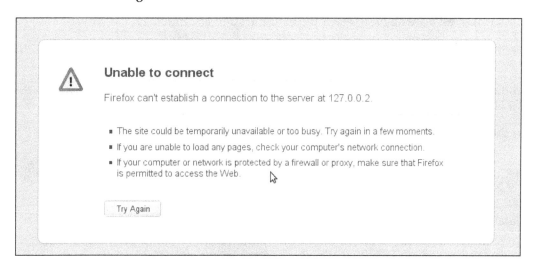

In such a situation, the first thing to check would be the status of the Apache2 server.

Let's run the command:

```
koha@linux:~ # sudo /etc/init.d/apache2 status
Checking for httpd2:                                        unused
```

If Apache2 is not running, run this command to bring the server up:

```
koha@linux:~ # sudo /etc/init.d/apache2 start
Starting httpd2 (prefork)
done
```

A common reason for Apache2 being down, especially on openSuSE and similar distributions' is that the machine has been rebooted, and Apache2 has not been configured to start up at boot time.

To test if this is the case, we use the command chkconfig:

```
koha@linux:/home/koha # sudo chkconfig apache2
apache2  off
```

To make sure Apache2 starts at boot, we use the `chkconfig` command with the `on` option:

```
koha@linux:~ # sudo chkconfig apache2 on
```

Let's run a test once again to see if the configuration is correct:

```
koha@linux:/home/koha # sudo chkconfig apache2
apache2   on
```

There could be other reasons for the problem, of course; look at the Apache2 log files for clues. To view or track the log file, we use the `tail` command:

```
koha@linux:/home/koha # tail -f /var/log/apache2/error_log
```

MySQL database server is down

If the MySQL database server is down, you will not be able to connect to the database. You should see something like this:

Koha error

The following fatal error has occurred:

```
Can't connect to local MySQL server through socket '/var/run/mysql/mysql.sock' (2) at /usr/share/kohaclone/C4/Context.pm line 666.
Compilation failed in require at /usr/share/kohaclone/C4/Circulation.pm line 25.
BEGIN failed--compilation aborted at /usr/share/kohaclone/C4/Circulation.pm line 25.
Compilation failed in require at /usr/share/kohaclone/C4/Overdues.pm line 24.
BEGIN failed--compilation aborted at /usr/share/kohaclone/C4/Overdues.pm line 24.
Compilation failed in require at /usr/share/kohaclone/C4/Members.pm line 27.
BEGIN failed--compilation aborted at /usr/share/kohaclone/C4/Members.pm line 27.
Compilation failed in require at /usr/share/kohaclone/C4/Auth.pm line 27.
BEGIN failed--compilation aborted at /usr/share/kohaclone/C4/Auth.pm line 27.
Compilation failed in require at /usr/share/kohaclone/opac/opac-main.pl line 22.
BEGIN failed--compilation aborted at /usr/share/kohaclone/opac/opac-main.pl line 22.
```

In such a situation, the first thing to check is if the MySQL database server is running or not. To test status of MySQL, we run the `status` command as follows:

```
koha@linux:~ # sudo /etc/init.d/mysql status
```
```
Checking for service MySQL:                                        unused
```

The unused message above indicates that MySQL is down. To bring the database server up, we execute the start command:

```
koha@linux:~ # sudo /etc/init.d/mysql start
Starting service MySQL                                        done
```

As with Apache2 on openSuSE and similar distributions, MySQL may not have been configured to start up at boot time.

To test if this is the case, we run command chkconfig:

```
koha@linux:/home/koha # sudo chkconfig mysql
mysql   off
```

To make sure MySQL starts at boot, we run chkconfig with the on option:

```
koha@linux:~ # sudo chkconfig  mysql  on
```

Again, just like with Apache2, let's run a test once again to make sure the configuration is correct:

```
koha@linux:/home/koha # sudo chkconfig mysql
mysql     on
```

There could be other reasons for the problem; you might want to take a look at the MySQL logs for clues:

```
koha@linux:/home/koha # tail -f /var/log/mysql/mysqld.log
```

The messages log file is a general system log file, and may contain useful information as well:

```
koha@linux:/home/koha # tail -f /var/log/messages
```

Zebra search not returning any results

Another common problem is Zebra searches don't return any results.

The **No Result found** message looks perfectly innocuous. Maybe you don't have a match for the search term. But if this happens for search terms you know should return results, then the first thing you should look at is the Zebra server.

	Log in to Your Account
My OPAC Header	

koha Search [Library Catalog ∨] [a   ] [Go]   🛒 Cart   Lists ▾

Advanced Search | Browse by Hierarchy | Browse by Subject | Most Popular

No Result found !

No results match your search for "a" in My Library Name Catalog. 📶

My OPAC Credits

Languages: English | hindi

We use the `ps` command to see if `zebrasrv` is running:

```
koha@linux:/home/koha # ps -eaf|grep zebra
root      2032  1540  0 14:38 pts/0    00:00:00 grep zebra
```

In this case, there is no `zebrasrv` process. To fix the problem, we need to start up the Zebra server. We execute the `zebrasrv` command like this:

```
koha@linux:/home/koha # zebrasrv -f /etc/koha-dev/etc/koha-conf.xml &
```

Or, if we have the Zebra daemon service setup, we start the server like this:

```
linux-4yut:/home/koha # sudo /etc/init.d/koha-zebra-daemon start
```

Let's test if the server is up, again using the `ps` command:

```
koha@linux:/home/koha # ps -eaf|grep zebra
root      2033  1540  0 14:39 pts/0    00:00:00 zebrasrv -f /etc/koha-
dev/etc/koha-conf.xml
root      2046  1540  0 14:39 pts/0    00:00:00 grep zebra
```

The output this time tells us that there is an active `zebrasrv` process.

A common reason for the Zebra server being down is that it is not configured to start up when the machines reboots.

On Debian, we use the `update-rc.d` command to set this up:

```
linux-4yut:/home/koha # sudo update-rc.d koha-zebra-daemon defaults
```

On openSuSE, we use the `chkconfig` command to set this up:

```
koha@linux:/home/koha # sudo chkconfig koha-zebra-daemon on
```

On openSuSE, if you are not using the `koha-zebra-daemon` service, you can setup the `zebrasrv` command in the `/etc/init.d/boot.local` file. Edit the `boot.local` file:

```
koha@linux:~> sudo vi /etc/init.d/boot.local
```

And add the `zebrasrv` command to the file somewhere near the end of the file, as follows:

```
/usr/bin/zebrasrv -f /etc/koha-dev/etc/koha-conf.xml &
```

There could be several reasons for the server coming down; look at the Zebra server log file for clues:

```
koha@linux:/home/koha # tail -f /etc/koha-dev/var/log/zebrasrv.log
```

For more information on configuring a Zebra server, see *Chapter 4, Koha's Web Installer, Crontab, and Other Server Configurations*.

Zebra index rebuild not working

You should know there is a problem with the rebuild process when changes to catalog items — new records, edits to records, or changes in checkout statuses do not reflect properly in search results on the OPAC and in the Staff Client.

The rebuild process may not be running due to several reasons.

If the rebuild process is setup correctly in the Crontab, you should see something like this in the messages log:

```
koha@linux:/home/koha # tail -f /var/log/messages
Jun  3 16:14:01 koha@linux /usr/sbin/cron[4010]: (root) CMD (/home/koha/
kohaclone/misc/migration_tools/rebuild_zebra.pl -b -a -z >> /home/koha/
logs/zebra.log  2>&1
)
```

If you do not see `rebuild_zebra.pl` executing in the log file, then you know that there is problem with the Crontab configuration.

To view how the Crontab is setup, we use the `crontab` command with the `-l` option:

```
koha@linux:/home/koha # crontab -l
```

A properly configured Crontab will look something like this:

```
PERL5LIB=/home/koha/kohaclone
KOHA_CONF=/etc/koha-dev/etc/koha-conf.xml
*/1 * * * * perl /home/koha/kohaclone/misc/migration_tools/rebuild_
zebra.pl -b -a -z >> /home/koha/logs/zebra.log  2>&1
```

It is important to set up the environment variables `PERL5LIB` and `KOHA_CONF` in the Crontab.

For more clues, you should refer to the rebuild log file:

```
koha@linux:/home/koha # tail -f /etc/koha-dev/var/log/rebuild_zebra.log
```

For more information on configuring Zebra's index rebuild in the Crontab, see *Chapter 4, Koha's Web Installer, Crontab, and Other Server Configurations.*

Parser problems

If you are using non-English characters—Spanish or French, then the SAX parser is something you will need to have setup correctly.

A search expression matching a record that has such characters in any field will result in an error like this:

In this type of situation, you should check the SAX parser setting. We do this by executing Koha's SAX parser print program /misc/sax_parser_print.pl:

```
koha@koha@linux:~> cd /home/koha/kohaclone/misc/
koha@linux:/home/koha/kohaclone/misc # ./sax_parser_print.pl
Koha wants something like:
    XML::LibXML::SAX::Parser=HASH(0x81fe220)
You have:
    XML::LibXML::SAX=HASH(0x834fea4)
Looks bad, check INSTALL.* documentation.
```

The error **looks bad** indicates that the configured parser is not suitable for Koha use. To correct this problem, we edit the parser's initialization file:

```
koha@linux:/home/koha/kohaclone/misc # vi /usr/lib/perl5/vendor_
perl/5.10.0/XML/SAX/ParserDetails.ini
```

And, replace [XML::SAX::PurePerl] or [XML::SAX::Expat], as the case may be, with [XML::LibXML::SAX::Parser].

For more information on configuring the SAX parser, see *Chapter 4, Koha's Web Installer, Crontab, and Other Server Configurations.*

Overdues e-mail not working

In our experience, problems related to overdue notice e-mails are fairly common. This is a more complex problem to troubleshoot, as there are a whole set of things that need to be in place.

Reviewing notice triggers

Overdue notices may not work correctly if they are not setup correctly in the **Notice/status triggers** section under **Tools**. Make sure the **Letter** and **Delay** is setup correctly for the **Patron Category** in question.

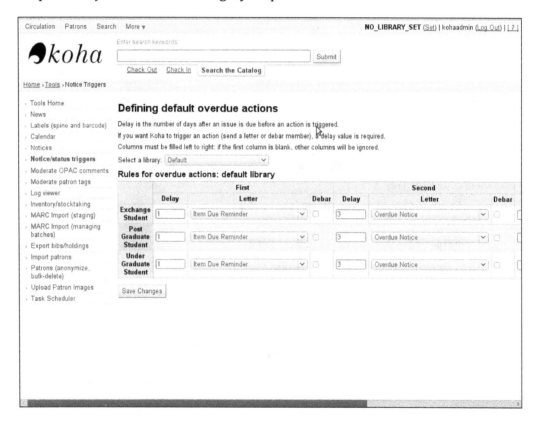

Troubleshooting e-mail problems

Next, we look at the **Messaging** tab of the Patron who is not receiving overdue messages. If there are messages in the **Pending** status, we know there is a problem with e-mailing messages, rather than generation of notices.

Let's first look at the status of the mail server:

```
koha@linux:/home/koha # rcpostfix status
Checking for service
Postfix:                                    running
```

We should also try to send an e-mail from the Linux shell:

```
koha@linux:/home/koha # mail -s "Hello Koha"
```

```
myemail@mydomain.com
EOT
```

If both these steps are working, we need to look at the messages log file to make sure that the cronjob for the process_message_queue.pl program is running:

```
koha@linux:/home/koha # tail -f /var/log/messages
```

```
May 31 09:55:01 koha@linux /usr/sbin/cron[8980]: (koha) CMD (perl /home/
koha/kohaclone/bin/cronjobs/process_message_queue.pl)
```

To view how the Crontab is setup, we use the `crontab` command with the `-l` option:

```
koha@linux:/home/koha # crontab -l
```

A properly configured Crontab will have the Koha-related environment variables setup:

```
PERL5LIB=/home/koha/kohaclone
KOHA_CONF=/etc/koha-dev/etc/koha-conf.xml
```

And, the `cronjob` should be setup as follows:

```
30 6 * * * perl /home/koha/kohaclone/bin/cronjobs/process_message_queue.pl
```

For more clues, run the `process_message_queue.pl` program from the Linux shell in verbose mode using the `-v` option:

```
koha@linux:/home/koha/kohaclone/misc/cronjobs # perl process_message_queue.pl  -v
```

Troubleshooting problems with generation of notices

If you don't see any **pending** messages in the messaging tab, then there could be a problem with the Cronjob for the `overdue_notices.pl` program.

First, it might be a good idea to look at the `messages` log file to see if the program is running:

```
koha@linux:/home/koha # tail -f /var/log/messages
May 31 09:45:01 koha@linux /usr/sbin/cron[8792]: (koha) CMD (perl /home/koha/kohaclone/bin/cronjobs/overdue_notices.pl -t)
```

A properly configured Crontab will have the Koha-related environment variables setup, and a Cronjob for the `overdue_notices.pl` program:

```
koha@linux:/home/koha # crontab -l

...

PERL5LIB=/home/koha/kohaclone
KOHA_CONF=/etc/koha-dev/etc/koha-conf.xml

. . .

45 5 * * * perl /home/koha/kohaclone/bin/cronjobs/overdue_notices.pl -t
```

If the Crontab configuration is fine, try running the `overdue_notices.pl` program from the Linux shell for clues:

```
koha@linux:/home/koha/kohaclone/misc/cronjobs # perl overdue_notices.pl
-v -t
```

Fines not working

Problems with fines calculations are fairly common as well.

Fines calculations may not work correctly if your fine rules are not setup correctly in the **Circulation and fine rules** section under **Koha Administration**. Make sure that the **Fine Amount** is setup correctly for the **Patron Category** and **Item Type** in question.

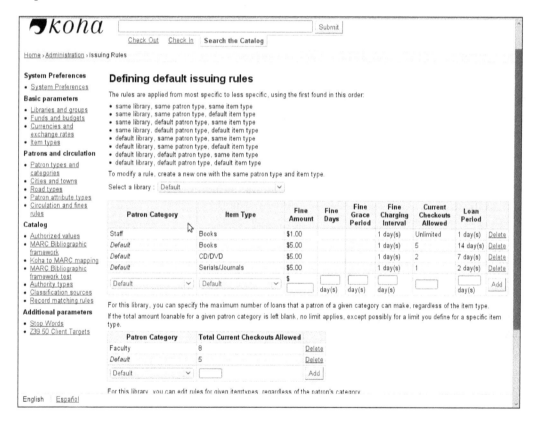

Another common mistake is to neglect to change the system preference from *finesmode* to *production*.

You might also want to make sure that the `fines.pl` program is setup in the correctly in the Crontab:

```
koha@linux:/home/koha # tail -f /var/log/messages
Jul 14 10:05:01 koha@linux /usr/sbin/cron[7741]: (root) CMD
perl /home/koha/kohaclone/bin/cronjobs/fines.pl)
```

A properly configured Crontab will have the Koha-related environment variables setup, and a Cronjob for the `fines.pl` program:

```
koha@linux:/home/koha # crontab -l

...

PERL5LIB=/home/koha/kohaclone

KOHA_CONF=/etc/koha-dev/etc/koha-conf.xml

. . .

0 7 * * * perl /home/koha/kohaclone/bin/cronjobs/fines.pl
```

For more clues, try running the `fines.pl` program from the Linux shell:

```
koha@linux:/home/koha/kohaclone/misc/cronjobs # perl fines.pl
Fines assessment -- 2010-07-17 -- Saved to /tmp/koha_2010-07-17.log
Number of Overdue Items:
    counted 1
   reported 1
```

The program outputs information into a log file, which might contain interesting information:

```
koha@linux:/home/koha/kohaclone/misc/cronjobs # vi /tmp/koha_2010-07-
17.log
cardnumber      categorycode    surname firstname        email    phone
 address citystate       itemnumber      barcode date_due         type
 days_overdue    fine
1       S       Sirohi  Savitra myemail@mydomain.com
12345678        My Address 1            1       30108000050959
2010-07-14              3       3
```

Software bugs

Sometimes, you may come across software bugs. You can raise such issues in Koha's bug tracker. Often, you will find that someone has already raised a bug report, and a fix is available as well.

Here is an example of a bug report on the tracker:

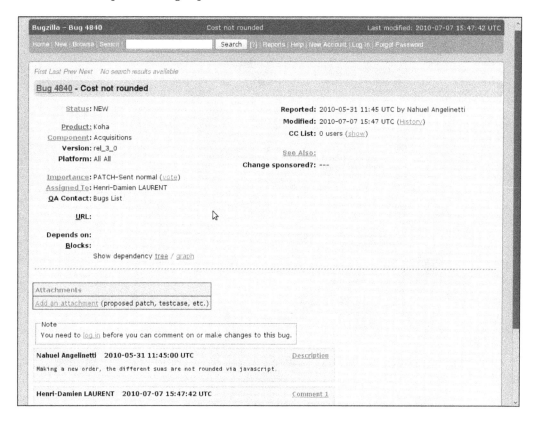

If a bug fix is available, and if Koha's release manager has pushed the fix into the repository, you will find the patch in Koha's Git repository.

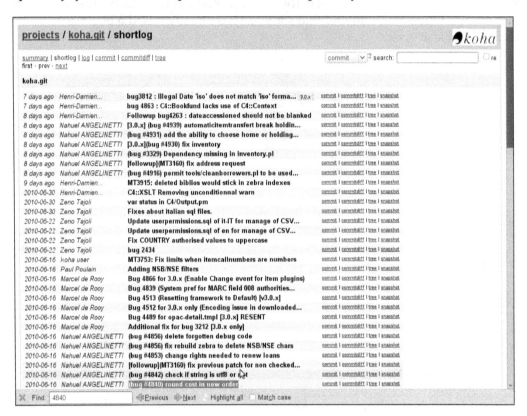

To apply the fix to our installation, we use the `git pull` command, something like this:

```
koha@linux:/home/koha/kohaclone # git pull origin 3.0.x
```

This command will pull the bug fix, along, with all the other changes in the repository since the last pull. We will learn more about `git pull` in the next chapter, *Chapter 11, Updating Software*.

If a bug fix is available, but has not been pushed into the Koha repository, you can download the patch from the bug reports, and try to apply it yourself. To apply a patch, we use the command `git apply`:

```
koha@linux:/home/koha/kohaclone # git apply name-of-patch.patch
```

Command line programs—environment variables not exported

If you don't have Koha's environment variables set up correctly for the Linux shell, you will see errors like this when running command-line programs, such as `bulkmarcimport.pl`:

```
1i85-160:/home/koha/kohaclone/misc/migration_tools # perl bulkmarcimport.
pl --h
Can't locate C4/Context.pm in @INC (@INC contains: /usr/lib/perl5/5.10.0/
i586-linux-thread-multi /usr/lib/perl5/5.10.0 /usr/lib/perl5/site_
perl/5.10.0/i586-linux-thread-multi /usr/lib/perl5/site_perl/5.10.0 /
usr/lib/perl5/vendor_perl/5.10.0/i586-linux-thread-multi /usr/lib/perl5/
vendor_perl/5.10.0 /usr/lib/perl5/vendor_perl .) at bulkmarcimport.pl
line 21.
BEGIN failed--compilation aborted at bulkmarcimport.pl line 21.
```

To avoid this problem, we need to export the KOHA_CONF and PERL5LIB environment variables:

```
koha@linux:/home/koha/kohaclone # export KOHA_CONF=/etc/koha-dev/etc/
koha-conf.xml
koha@linux:/home/koha/kohaclone# export PERL5LIB=/home/koha/kohaclone
```

To set these up to be persistent across sessions, we add these lines to the `/etc/bash.bashrc` file in Debian, and to the `/etc/bash.bashrc.local` file in openSuSE.

Problems with Internet Explorer

Some Koha screens may not display properly in Microsoft's Internet explorer:

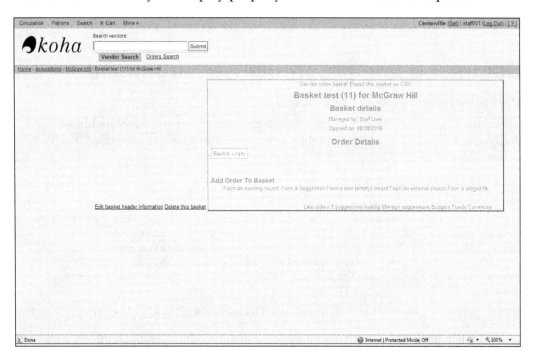

You can try looking for a fix in the Koha bug tracker or in its Git repository. It is best, however, if you use Firefox, Chrome, or other browsers; things should be just fine on those.

Summary

In this chapter, we learned how to troubleshoot application problems. Koha's community tools — mailing lists, IRC chat, Git repository, and bugs repository — are a great help.

To get you started on Koha troubleshooting skills, we walked you through troubleshooting tasks for some common problems with Apache2, MySQL, and Zebra.

We learned how to tackle more complex problems related to overdue notices e-mails, fines, and finding and applying bug fix patches.

We also learned the importance of exporting Koha's environment variables, and of setting up the SAX parser correctly.

In the next chapter, we will learn how to download and install software updates.

11
Updating Software

The Koha software is always changing, almost every day. These changes contain bug fixes, minor revisions to existing features, and entirely new features. You should keep the software updated to benefit from these changes.

Even if the new versions do not contain changes of interest to you, it is good practice to keep the software updated. If your version falls too far behind the current version, the update process to the latest version is likely to be very difficult.

In this chapter we learn how to download and install software updates. We cover the chapter in two steps—an orientation followed by a demonstration of the process.

Orientation to updating software

Before we can update the Koha software, let us learn about Koha's software versions and how to choose the version to upgrade to. In this section we also learn about the components of a software update, and how to install each component of the update properly.

Understanding Koha's software versions

To choose which new version to upgrade to, let us first understand how the Koha software is organized.

Branches

At any given point Koha has at least two main software branches:

- Stable: This branch is older and is considered stable or bug free for the most part. Only bug fixes are allowed on this branch.
- Development: This branch is where new features are developed. This branch is ahead of the stable branch, meaning it has all the features of the stable branch and the new features in development.

Heads

Both branches – stable and development have heads. A heads is the tip of the branch, pointing to the latest change made in that branch.

At the time of writing of this chapter, there are two heads available in Koha's Git repository.

- 3.0.x: This is the tip of the stable branch
- master: This is the tip of the development branch

Tags

Both branches have multiple tags. Tags point to specific points in a branch's change history. For instance we see these tags related to the stable branch:

- v3.00.06: This is the latest stable branch
- v3.00.05: An earlier version of the 3.0.x branch
- v3.00.04: An earlier version of the 3.0.x branch
- v3.00.03: An earlier version of the 3.0.x branch

And these tags are available for the development branch:

- v3.02.00-beta: This is the 3.02 branch in the beta testing stage
- v3.03.00-alpha: This is the 3.02 branch when released for alpha testing

Choosing a version to update to

We can choose to move to the head of the stable branch or the head of the development branch or to any tag in one of these branches.

Here are some pointers to help you decide:

- On production servers, we upgrade to the latest stable tag in the stable branch
- To take an early look at new features being developed, switch to the alpha or beta tag in the development branch, if available
- If you want to take a look at the very latest version of the software, switch to head of the development branch

Understanding components of software updates

When bugs are fixed or new features are added in Koha, different types of files and programs can change such as these:

- Perl, Java script, HTML, CSS, and other types of files in `kohaclone` folder
- Tables, columns, constraints, indexes, system preferences, and other types of changes in Koha's database
- Indexes and properties in Zebra configuration files
- Directives in Koha's Apache2 configuration files

An overview of the installation process

To ensure that software updates are installed properly, we need to follow these steps:

- **Download software updates**: We can download updates using Git. Git automatically detects our current version and downloads updates from Koha's online repository.
- **Switch to a specific software version**: Depending on our purposes, we will choose a version that we want to upgrade to.
- **Install Perl module prerequisites**: The new version of the software may depend on new Perl modules; we will need to install these.
- **Install the new version of Koha**: We will install the new Koha version using the make utility; this process is similar to that of a fresh Koha install.

- **Configure Apache2**: The new version of the software may have an updated Apache2 configuration file. We will need to configure this new file.

- **Upgrade the database**: We will use Koha's web installer to upgrade the database to the new version.

- **Rebuild Zebra indexes**: The new software version may contain updates to Zebra configuration files. To have these changes reflected in search results, we will need to do a full rebuild of Zebra's indexes.

- **Restart Zebra server**: To load new Zebra configurations we will have to restart zebrasrv.

Updating the software

Now that we have an understanding of how to update the software, let us go ahead and execute the update process.

Downloading updates using git pull command

To download software updates, we use the git pull command. Before we do that let us check what branch we are on at this time by using the git branch command:

```
koha@li190-245:~/kohaclone$ git branch
* koha-3.0.2
  master
```

This * in the output above indicates that we are on the 3.0.2 version, which at the time of writing is an older version on Koha's stable branch.

Let us also check the branches on the online Koha repository, by using the git branch command with the -r (for remote branch) option:

```
koha@li190-245:~/kohaclone$ git branch -r
  origin/3.0.x
  origin/HEAD -> origin/master
  origin/biblibre-acq-preview-only
  origin/biblibre-integration
  origin/biblibre-sopac
  origin/labels_recon
  origin/master
  origin/new/bug3987_alpha_sysprefs
  origin/new_features
  origin/rfid-direct-tagging
  origin/sysprefs_editor
```

Of the several branches listed in the output above, two are of immediate interest to us—origin/3.0.x and origin/HEAD or origin/master. Origin/3.0.x is the stable branch while origin/HEAD or origin/master is the development branch.

If we are on a production server and we are interested only in updates for the stable branch, we will run the git pull command pointing to the stable branch—origin/3.0.x:

koha@li190-245:~/kohaclone$ git pull origin 3.0.x

If we are on a test machine, and we want to upgrade to the development branch for development of test purposes, we run the git pull command pointing to the development branch—origin/master:

koha@li190-245:~/kohaclone$ git pull origin master

Once the command is executed your Koha server has the latest updates available in the kohaclone folder.

Switching to a new software version

Now we need to decide which version of the software to use, this of course depends on what your purpose of upgrading is.

First let us take a look at the tags that are available. To determine this, we use the command git tag:

koha@li190-245:~/kohaclone$ git tag

We see several tags, at the bottom of the list; you should see tags for the 3.0.x branch, something like this:

v3.00.03

v3.00.04

v3.00.05

v3.00.06

And at the very bottom, tags for the master branch, which is currently versioned 3.02.xx:

v3.02.00-alpha

v3.02.00-alpha2

v3.02.00-beta

To switch to the master or the head of the branch, we run the `git checkout` command as follows:

```
koha@li190-245:~/kohaclone$ git checkout master
```

We see from the output of the `git tag` command that the latest tag or version in Koha's stable branch is version `v3.00.06`. To switch to this version, we would run the `git checkout` command with the `-b` option and with a label for the new branch and the tag as parameters:

```
koha@li190-245:~/kohaclone$ git checkout -b <label for the new branch>
<tag pointing to the version>
```

The `-b` option creates a new branch with the specified label and points the branch to the software version specified by the tag. This command would be executed like this:

```
koha@li190-245:~/kohaclone$ git checkout -b koha-3.0.6 v3.00.06
```

To switch to tag `3.02.00-beta` on the development branch, we would run the `git checkout` command as follows:

```
koha@li190-245:~/kohaclone$ git checkout -b koha-3.02-beta v3.02.00-beta
```

To test if you have switched branches successfully, use the `git branch` command:

```
koha@li190-245:~/kohaclone$ git branch
* koha-3.02-beta
  master
```

Installing the new software version

Once we have switched to the software version we want to use, we will install the new Koha version in the same way that we do a fresh Koha install. The reader should refer to *Chapters 1* and *2* for help with these steps.

Running the Makefile.PL program

First we run the `Makefile.PL` program. As this is a software update and not a fresh install, we need to make sure we enter configuration details corresponding to the current installation:

```
linux-4yut:/usr/share/kohaclone # perl Makefile.PL
```

We chose the `dev` installation mode during our initial installation; make sure we choose the same here:

```
Installation mode (dev, single, standard) [standard] dev
```

Set the `configuration directory` to the directory configuration directory of the current installation:

```
Configuration directory: [/home/koha/koha-dev]
```

Make sure to specify the current database name here:

```
Please specify the name of the database to be used by Koha [koha]
```

Specify the MySQL user that has privileges over the database:

```
Please specify the user that owns the database to be used by Koha
[kohaadmin]
```

Specify the password of this MySQL user:

```
Please specify the password of the user that owns the database to be used
by Koha [katikoan] katikoan
```

If you are using Zebra, say yes here:

```
Install the Zebra configuration files? (no, yes) [yes]
```

For other questions, the default value should be fine. Simply press the *Return* key to proceed to the next step.

Installing Perl modules

The `Makefile.PL` step above may end with warnings on missing Perl module prerequisites:

```
[Mon Jun 14 16:12:27 2010] Makefile.PL: Warning: prerequisite IPC::Cmd
0.46 not found. We have 0.401.
[Mon Jun 14 16:12:30 2010] Makefile.PL: Warning: prerequisite
Text::CSV::Encoded 0.09 not found.
Writing Makefile for koha
linux-4yut:/usr/share/kohaclone #
```

We will need to install these missing modules using the package manager or the CPAN shell. Refer to *Chapter 1* for more information on how to install Perl modules.

Completing Koha installation

Once all Perl modules are installed successfully, we finish the installation of the new version by running the rest of the `make` commands:

```
koha@li190-245:~/kohaclone$ make

koha@li190-245:~/kohaclone$ make test

koha@li190-245:~/kohaclone$ sudo make install
```

Configuring Apache2

Installation of the new Koha version will overwrite Koha's Apache2 configuration file—/etc/koha-dev/etc/koha-httpd.conf. This is why we will need to configure Apache2 once again. Refer to *Chapter 2* for more information on how to configure Apache2.

Upgrading the database

Once we have Apache2 configured we navigate to Koha's staff client to launch Koha's web installer. Here we use the kohaadmin MySQL user to log on.

Once we log in, we see a database upgrade message. In this step the installer will upgrade the database to match the new version of the software.

Once the database upgrade finishes, you should be able to log in to the new version of Koha.

Zebra—rebuilding indexes and restarting the server

As a final step we need to do a full rebuild of Zebra indexes in line with the new Zebra configuration files. We also restart `zebrasrv` to load the new configurations.

Rebuilding Zebra indexes

We run the `rebuild_zebra.pl` program with the `-r` option to do a full rebuild:

```
Linux-4yut:/usr/share/kohaclone # ./misc/migration_tools/rebuild_zebra.pl
-b -a -r -v
Restart Zebrasrv
```

Restarting zebrasrv

To restart `zebrasrv`, we restart the Zebra daemon as follows:

```
linux-4yut:/home/koha # sudo /etc/init.d/koha-zebra-daemon restart
```

Summary

Here is what we learned in this chapter on updating software:

- Using `git pull` command to download software updates
- Using `git branch` command to switch to a specific software version
- Installing the new Koha version using the Make utility
- Upgrading the database using Koha's web installer
- Rebuilding Zebra indexes using new Zebra configuration files
- Restarting Zebra server to load new configurations

In the next chapter, we will learn about a related topic—how to make your own modifications to the Koha software.

12
Customizing Koha Software

Most serious Koha users will want to customize the software to suit their needs, perhaps to modify the styling or appearance or to tweak a certain page to show additional information. If you have the skills, you can even take on more serious work, such adding new features.

It is best to share the code you create by sending patches to Koha's release manager. Koha's license requires that we share any enhancements we make. Another reason to share the code is that if your changes are included in upcoming releases, you don't have to do the work of retrofitting your changes into the new version.

In this chapter, we learn how to customize Koha code. We start with an orientation, and then use a specific example to demonstrate how to implement and share software changes.

An orientation to customizing Koha software

Let's first get an understanding on how to go about customizing software. We will learn about the skills required, the organization of Koha's application folder and its database, and the process of making the software changes using Git, Koha's version-control system.

Skills needed

Here is a quick overview of the skills needed to customize Koha. If you want to modify styling and appearance, HTML and CSS skills should suffice. If you want to work on more complex features, you will likely need JavaScript, Perl, and SQL skills as well:

- HTML: Koha runs in a browser, basic HTML skills are required if you want to make changes to Koha's screens

- CSS: Size, fonts, position, or colors on Koha screens are controlled via CSS files

- JavaScript: JavaScript adds interactivity to web pages; in Koha, JavaScript is used for tasks such as validating keyed data or building menus

- Perl: Koha's scripting language. If you need to work outside of basic styling and appearance changes, you will need Perl skills

- SQL: Along with Perl, you will need SQL skills to access or modify data in the database

Understanding Koha's application folder

To be able to make changes to the software, we need to understand the structure of Koha's application folder — how the folders are organized, what they contain, and how the different file types are related to each other.

Top level folders

Here is a description of the some of the important folders in the `kohaclone` folder:

- `C4`: This folder contains Koha's Perl modules. These Perl modules are shared libraries, containing subroutines that are used by various Perl scripts throughout the Koha application.

- `etc`: This folder contains Apache2, Zebra, and Koha's configuration files.

- `installer`: This folder contains Koha's web installer files, including those that install or upgrade the Koha database.

- `koha-tmpl`: This folder contains files related to staff client and OPAC screens.

- Perl scripts: Koha's Perl scripts are organized by function in folders, such as `acqui` — for acquisitions, `circ` — for circulations, or `misc` — for various command-line and Crontab programs.

Template files

Let's take a closer look at the `koha-tmpl` file; this folder contains files and folders related to Koha's screens:

- The `koha-tmpl` folder contains two folders—`opac-tmpl` for the OPAC, and `intranet-tmpl` for the staff client

- The OPAC and staff client template folder each contains a theme folder named `prog`

- The theme folder in turn contains a language folder—`en` or `fr`, depending how you installed Koha

- Within the language folder, you will find a set of folders `js`—containing JavaScript files, includes—header, footer, masthead and other include files, `lib`—external display-related libraries, such as `yui` and `jquery`, `modules`—template files that display Koha's pages and `css`—stylesheets

Relationships between different types of files

Let's understand how Perl scripts, Perl modules, and template files are related:

- Perl scripts call or use subroutines in Perl modules. To use a subroutine, the Perl script must first load the module using the Use statement, like this:

  ```
  use C4::Items;
  ```

- Perl scripts, especially those that are used in Koha screens, have one or more template files associated with them. To see which template file is associated, look for statements such as this:

  ```
   = get_template_and_user({template_name => "cataloguing/additem.
  tmpl",
  ```

- Template files include header or footer types of include files using a statement such as this:

  ```
  <!-- TMPL_INCLUDE NAME="doc-head-open.inc" -->
  ```

- CSS and JavaScript files are usually included in template files via the include file `doc-head-close.inc`

Understanding Koha's database

We also need to understand how Koha's database is organized. This will help us make software changes that require access to the database or that require updates to be made to it. In this section we take a quick look at how to browse the database; we also list some of the important tables.

Browsing Koha's database

Let's start by logging in to MySQL. First, we use the `use` command to switch to Koha's database:

```
mysql> use koha
Database changed
```

We use the `show tables` command to view a listing of all tables in the database:

```
mysql> show tables;
+-----------------------------------------+
| Tables_in_koha_testing                  |
+-----------------------------------------+
| accountlines                            |
| accountoffsets                          |
| action_logs                             |
| alert                                   |
| aqbasket                                |
| aqbookfund                              |
| aqbooksellers                           |
```

To view how a particular table organized, we use the `describe` command:

```
mysql> describe borrowers;
+---------------------+-------------+------+-----+---------+------------
----+
| Field               | Type        | Null | Key | Default | Extra
|
+---------------------+-------------+------+-----+---------+------------
----+
| borrowernumber      | int(11)     | NO   | PRI | NULL    | auto_
increment |
```

cardnumber	varchar(16)	YES	UNI	NULL	
surname	mediumtext	NO		NULL	
firstname	text	YES		NULL	

An overview of important Koha tables

Here is a quick overview of some of the important tables in Koha, categorized by function.

Cataloguing

The following three tables are key Cataloguing related tables:

- `biblio`: Contains bibliographic data such as title or author.
- `biblioitems`: Also contains bibliographic data; there is one-to-one correspondence between records in `biblio` and `biblioitems` tables. This table stores the MARC record in the field `marcxml`
- `items`: Contains holdings records.

Circulation

Here is a listing of important circulation-related tables:

- `issues`: Contains current checkouts
- `old_issues`: Contains items that have been checked in
- `reserves`: Contains open hold requests
- `old_reserves`: Contains hold requests that are cancelled or fulfilled

Patrons

Here are two key patrons-related tables:

- `borrowers`: Contains patron records
- `accountlines`: Contains data on patrons fines and other dues

Administration

Administrative setting and data are stored in the following tables:

- `libraries`: Libraries participating in the system
- `itemtypes`: Item types are used in circulation rules
- `categories`: Patron categories
- `issuingrules`: Circulation and fine rules
- `systempreferences`: Global system preferences
- `aqbookfund`: Funds, budgets are created under funds
- `aqbudget`: Budgets under each fund

Serials

Serials data is captured in the following tables:

- `subscription`: Subscription information such as frequency, numbering pattern, start and end dates
- `subscriptionhistory`: Table that tracks missing and received issues
- `serial`: Table connecting bibliographic records and subscriptions
- `serialitems`: Items under a serial record

Acquisitions

Acquisitions-related data is captured under these tables:

- `aqbasket`: Contains order baskets
- `aqbooksellers`: Table containing vendor records
- `aqorders`: Contains orders within a basket
- `aqorderdelivery`: Contains records of shipments received
- `aqorderbreakdown`: Contains information on budget utilization against each order

Koha's database structure

Here is a useful diagram of the database structure including key tables, their columns, and relationships between the tables:

`http://wiki.koha-community.org/wiki/File:Kohastructure.png`

Using Git to manage software changes

It is highly recommended that the software changes be managed using Git. Some of the benefits of using Git are:

- Make changes safely in a separate development branch
- Undo changes easily, even if changes are to a large number of files
- Automatically merge your changes with those available in Koha's online repositories
- Share your changes with others, including Koha's release manager

Here is a listing of some Git commands we will use:

- `git checkout`: To create a development branch.
- `git add`: Add one or more changed files to a commit.
- `git commit`: Records the changes along with a description or comment entered by the committer.
- `git format -patch`: Creates a patch—a file that contains all the changes in a single file. The patch can then be shared with others, including Koha's release manager. The release manager may choose to include the patch in upcoming versions of the software.
- `git send-email`: Sends an e-mail to Koha's release manager with the patch.
- For more information on Git commands, refer to these links:

  `http://git-scm.com/documentation`.

Understanding the software customization process

And finally, here is how we go about making a change:

- Creating a branch: As a first step, we use the `git checkout` command to create and switch to a new development branch. We can create one or more commits in this branch.
- Changing application files: We change one or more files using `vi` or other editors. These files may be Perl modules, Perl scripts, JavaScript, CSS, or template files.
- Making database changes: We make database changes in MySQL scripts in the installer folder.

- Changing configuration files: We make changes to Koha, Apache2, or Zebra configuration files in the `etc` folder.

- Creating a commit: Once all the changes related to a feature have been made, we commit the changes using the `git commit` command. The commit may consist of a single file or several files, but all files should be logically related.

- If we have changed any of configuration files in the `etc` folder, we install them using the `Makefile.PL`, `make`, and `make install` set of commands. These commands will install the new files in Koha's configuration folder, `/etc/koha-dev/etc/`.

- Changing the database: If we have made any database changes, we install these using Koha's web installer. The web installer runs automatically when we navigate to the staff client.

- Creating a patch: Once the changes are tested, we can use the `git format-patch` command to create a patch. The patch can be sent to Koha's release manager, or to others using the `git send-email` command.

Customizing Koha software—an example

Let's take a look at a specific example to understand how to modify Koha code.

Let's say we want to add the Google Indic Transliteration tool to the masthead on the OPAC. This tool transliterates text in the source language to a destination language selected from a drop-down list. The transliterated expression can be then be used as a search expression.

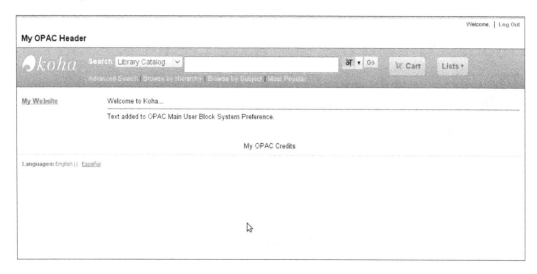

This feature requires the following changes:

- Modify the CSS file to position the transliteration control
- Modify the search box on the masthead to accept input in the source language
- Add the language selector drop-down list to the right of the search box
- Include a Google-provided JavaScript file; the transliteration is performed by this file
- Add a new system preference to control the availability of the tool

Creating a development branch

Let's first create a development branch in which to work by creating a copy of the master branch:

```
Koha@linux:/home/koha/kohaclone # git checkout -b mydevel master
```

This command creates a copy of the master branch, and switches to using this new branch.

Making CSS changes

To position the control via CSS, we edit the `opac.css` file in the `koha-tmpl/opac-tmpl/prog/en/css` folder:

```
koha@linux:/home/koha/kohaclone # vi koha-tmpl/opac-tmpl/prog/en/CSS/
opac.css
```

We add this block for the transliteration control to the CSS file:

```
#translControl{
float : left;
padding-left : .4em;
}
```

Creating a new JavaScript file

We create the new Google-provided JavaScript file in the folder `koha-tmpl/opac-tmpl/prog/en/js`. Open an empty new file using the `vi` command:

```
koha@linux:/home/koha/kohaclone # vi koha-tmpl/opac-tmpl/prog/en/js/
googleindictransliteration.js
```

And add the contents of the transliteration file to the file:

```
// Load the Google Transliteration API
google.load("elements", "1", {
    packages: "transliteration"
  });

function onLoad() {
  var options = {
```

Loading the Transliteration JavaScript file

Next, we add a block to load the transliteration JavaScript file. We add this block to the `doc-head-close.inc` file in the `koha-tmpl/opac-tmpl/prog/en/includes` folder. The `doc-head-close.inc` file is included in all OPAC pages, so we can be sure that our new JavaScript will be loaded in all pages.

koha@linux:/home/koha/kohaclone # vi koha-tmpl/opac-tmpl/prog/en/includes/doc-head-close.inc

We add this block to the include file:

```
<!-- TMPL_IF NAME="GoogleIndicTransliteration" -->
        <script type="text/JavaScript" src="http://www.google.com/
jsapi"></script>
        <script type="text/JavaScript" language="JavaScript" src="<!-
- TMPL_VAR NAME="themelang" -->/js/googleindictransliteration.js"></
script>
<!-- /TMPL_IF -->
```

Note the use of this if condition in the block above:

```
<!-- TMPL_IF NAME="GoogleIndicTransliteration" -->
```

This loads the Transliteration JavaScript only if a system preference **GoogleIndicTransliteration** is set to **On**.

Creating a system preference

Next, we create a system preference that will be used to control whether the transliteration tool will be displayed or not. The system preference once installed will look like this:

We will need to modify the database install and update scripts.

First, let's edit the `sysprefs.sql` file in the `installer/data/mysql/en/mandatory/` folder:

```
koha@linux:/home/koha/kohaclone # vi installer/data/mysql/en/
mandatory/sysprefs.sql
```

We add this block to the file:

```
INSERT INTO systempreferences (variable,value,explanation,options,ty
pe) VALUES ('GoogleIndicTransliteration','0','Allow display of Google
Indic Transliteration Tool in the OPAC Masthead',NULL,'YesNo');
```

The `sysprefs.sql` file is called from Koha's web installer. It is used to insert system preferences along with a description and a default value. This file is used only for fresh installations.

To make sure the new system preference is added when someone upgrades their Koha version, we need to add the following lines in the `updatebase30.pl` file in the folder `/installer/data/mysql/`:

```
koha@linux:/home/koha/kohaclone # vi installer/data/mysql/
updatedatabase30.pl
```

We add a block as follows at the bottom of the file. The field $DBversion is important; Koha's web installer, when deciding whether to upgrade the Koha database, checks if the database's current version is below the highest $DBversion value indicated in this file. If it is below this number, it initiates the database upgrade process.

Set the $DBversion by incrementing the last 3 digits of the number in the previous block in the file. So if the last block in the file starts with this line:

```
$DBversion = "3.00.06.010";
if (C4::Context->preference("Version") < TransformToNum($DBversion)) {
...

...
```

We create our new block as follows:

```
$DBversion = "3.00.06.011";
if (C4::Context->preference("Version") < TransformToNum($DBversion)) {
    $dbh->do("INSERT INTO systempreferences (variable,value,exp
lanation,options,type) VALUES ('GoogleIndicTransliteration','0'
,'Allow display of Google Indic Transliteration Tool in the OPAC
Masthead',NULL,'YesNo');");
    print "Upgrade to $DBversion done (Adding Google Indic
Transliteration Sys Pref)\n";
    SetVersion ($DBversion);
```

And finally, we edit the systempreferences.pl in the folder admin. This file controls the tab in which this new preference will be displayed in the Global System preferences module in Koha.

```
koha@linux:/home/koha/kohaclone # vi admin/systempreferences.pl
```

Add this line to show this preference in the OPAC tab in the Global System Preferences module in Koha:

```
$tabsysprefs{XSLTResultsDisplay}   = "OPAC";
```

Adding the transliteration tool to the display template

Next, we add the code to display the transliteration control on the OPAC pages. We add this block of code to the `masthead.inc` file in the folder `koha-tmpl/opac-tmpl/prog/en/includes/`. The `masthead.inc` file is included in all OPAC pages that have the **Search** tool on the top. Let's edit the file:

```
koha@linux:/home/koha/kohaclone # vi koha-tmpl/opac-tmpl/prog/en/
includes/masthead.inc
```

And, add this block of code:

```
<!-- TMPL_IF NAME="ms_value" -->
<input type="textbox" id = "transl1" name="q" value="<!-- TMPL_VAR
ESCAPE="HTML" NAME="ms_value" -->" class="left" style="width:35%;
font-size: 100%;"/><div id="translControl"></div>
<!-- TMPL_ELSE -->
<input type="textbox" id = "transl1" name="q" class="left"
style="width: 35%; font-size: 100%;"/><div id="translControl"></div>
```

Editing the Perl scripts to enable the system preference

And finally, we need a mechanism to look up the value (on or off) of the system preference in the database, and pass that value to the template files. We edit the `opac-main.pl` file in the folder `opac`:

```
koha@linux:/home/koha/kohaclone # vi opac/opac-main.pl
```

And add this block of code somewhere near the bottom of the file:

```
# If GoogleIndicTransliteration system preference is On Set parameter
to load Google's JavaScript in OPAC search screens
if (C4::Context->preference('GoogleIndicTransliteration')) {
        $template->param('GoogleIndicTransliteration' => 1);
}
```

Do the same in the `opac-search.pl` in the folder `opac`.

Committing changes

We will use Git to commit the changes we have just made. First, let's check what files are modified using the `git status` command:

```
koha@linux:/home/koha/kohaclone # git status
# On branch koha-3.0.2
# Changed but not updated:
#   (use "git add <file>..." to update what will be committed)
#   (use "git checkout -- <file>..." to discard changes in working
directory)
#
#       modified:   admin/systempreferences.pl
#       modified:   installer/data/mysql/en/mandatory/sysprefs.sql
#       modified:   installer/data/mysql/updatedatabase30.pl
#       modified:   koha-tmpl/opac-tmpl/prog/en/CSS/opac.CSS
#       modified:   koha-tmpl/opac-tmpl/prog/en/includes/doc-head-
...

...
```

Now, we add the specific files we want in the patch using the `git add` command:

```
koha@linux:/home/koha/kohaclone # git add admin/systempreferences.pl
koha@linux:/home/koha/kohaclone # git add installer/data/mysql/en/
mandatory/sysprefs.sql
koha@linux:/home/koha/kohaclone # git add installer/data/mysql/
updatedatabase30.pl

...

...
```

Once we have added all the files, we use the `git commit` command to make the commit:

```
koha@linux:/home/koha/kohaclone # git commit
```

The command prompts for user input; here we add a description of the commit:

```
    This adds the Google Indic Transliteration tool to the OPAC masthead.

# Please enter the commit message for your changes. Lines starting
# with '#' will be ignored, and an empty message aborts the commit.
#
```

```
# Committer: root <root@linux-4yut.site>
#
# On branch mydevel
# Changes to be committed:
#   (use "git reset HEAD <file>..." to unstage)
#
#       modified:   admin/systempreferences.pl
#       modified:   installer/data/mysql/en/mandatory/sysprefs.sql
...

...
```

Save the comment by using :wq, and the command should exit with a message such as this:

```
[mydevel 4727d7c] This adds the Google Indic Transliteration tool to the
OPAC masthead.
 9 files changed, 55 insertions(+), 3 deletions(-)
 create mode 100644 koha-tmpl/opac-tmpl/prog/en/js/
googleindictransliteration.js
```

To check if the commit was successful, we use the git log command:

```
koha@linux:/home/koha/kohaclone # git log
```

The output should display our commit on the top:

```
commit 4727d7ca977b032f08f0b67a6d0b9c778fdd386e
Author: root <root@linux-4yut.site>
Date:   Tue Jun 15 16:55:34 2010 +0530

    This adds the Google Indic Transliterater to the OPAC masthead.
```

Create a patch using Git

Now, let's say we have tested this change, and want to share it with others or send it to the Koha release manager for inclusion in upcoming Koha releases. To do this, we create a patch using the command git format-patch:

```
koha@linux:/home/koha/kohaclone # git format-patch origin/master
```

Note the use of the word `master` in the command above; this indicates that the patch should be created against the master branch. By doing this, we ensure that the patch can be applied on the master.

The command should exit by creating a single file containing all the changes:

`0001-This-adds-the-Google-Indic-Transliterater-to-the-OPA.patch`

Let's take a look at this file:

`koha@linux:/home/koha/kohaclone # cat 0001-This-adds-the-Google-Indic-Transliterater-to-the-OPA.patch`

The first few lines contain information, such as from, date and subject:

`From 4727d7ca977b032f08f0b67a6d0b9c778fdd386e Mon Sep 17 00:00:00 2001`

`From: root <root@linux-4yut.site>`

`Date: Tue, 15 Jun 2010 16:55:34 +0530`

`Subject: [PATCH] This adds the Google Indic Transliteration tool to the OPAC masthead`

The section below the information block gives a summary of the changes in terms of the files changes, and the number lines added or deleted:

```
admin/systempreferences.pl                             |    1 +
 installer/data/mysql/en/mandatory/sysprefs.sql        |    1 +
 installer/data/mysql/updatedatabase30.pl              |    5 +++
 koha-tmpl/opac-tmpl/prog/en/CSS/opac.CSS              |    5 +++
 .../opac-tmpl/prog/en/includes/doc-head-close.inc     |    4 +++
 koha-tmpl/opac-tmpl/prog/en/includes/masthead.inc     |    4 +-
 .../prog/en/js/googleindictransliteration.js          |   28
 +++++++++++++++++++++
 opac/opac-main.pl                                     |    5 +++
 opac/opac-search.pl                                   |    5 +++-
 9 files changed, 55 insertions(+), 3 deletions(-)
 create mode 100644 koha-tmpl/opac-tmpl/prog/en/js/
googleindictransliteration.js
```

And then, there blocks for each file that is changed; lines that are added are prefixed with a + sign, and those that are deleted are prefixed with a – sign.

`diff --git a/opac/opac-search.pl b/opac/opac-search.pl`

`index 7a0e3c8..d67dae7 100755`

`--- a/opac/opac-search.pl`

```
+++ b/opac/opac-search.pl
@@ -581,5 +581,8 @@ if (defined $barshelves) {
 }


 my $content_type = ($format eq 'rss' or $format eq 'atom') ? $format :
'html';
-

+# If GoogleIndicTransliteration system preference is On Set paramter to
load Google's JavaScript in OPAC search screens
+if (C4::Context->preference('GoogleIndicTransliteration')) {
+        $template->param('GoogleIndicTransliteration' => 1);
+}
 output_html_with_http_headers $cgi, $cookie, $template->output,
$content_type;
--
1.6.4.2
```

Sending the patch to Koha's release manager

To share your code, you can send the patch to the koha-patches list; Koha's release manager will then take a look at your code, and if it meets quality standards, include it in the appropriate branches.

To send the patch, first we setup our name and e-mail in Git:

```
koha@linux:/home/koha/kohaclone # git config --global user.name
"firstname lastname"
```

```
koha@linux:/home/koha/kohaclone # git config --global user.email
"myemail@mydomain.com"
```

To e-mail the patch, use the `git send-email` command:

```
koha@linux:/home/koha/kohaclone # git send-email 0001-This-adds-the-
Google-Indic-Transliterater-to-the-OPA.patch
```

The command will prompt for input; to the question `Who should the emails be sent to`, enter the e-mail address `koha-patches@lists.koha-community.org`:

```
Who should the emails be sent to? koha-patches@lists.koha-community.org
```

Summary

In this chapter on customizing Koha software, we learned about:

- The organization of Koha's application folder
- The structure of Koha's database
- How to make changes to configuration, database, and application files
- How to commit changes using Git
- How to generate patches using Git
- How to send patches to others using Git

In the next and final chapter, we will cover advanced topics, such as LDAP authentication, internationalization, and exposing the catalog to the outside world via the Z39.50 protocol.

13
Advanced Topics

In this final chapter, we will learn about setting up some less widely used but nevertheless important features of Koha. These features are:

- Creating and using one's own matching rules for catalog imports
- Authenticating users against an LDAP server
- Setting up custom OPAC interfaces for each library in your Koha installation
- Setting up Koha screens in other languages
- Publishing the catalog via Z39.50 protocol

Creating and using matching rules for use during catalog imports

Koha's default installation includes two record matching rules for use during catalog imports—one based on ISBN and the other for matching on ISSN. We can also create our own matching rules from the **Record Matching Rules** section under **Koha Administration**.

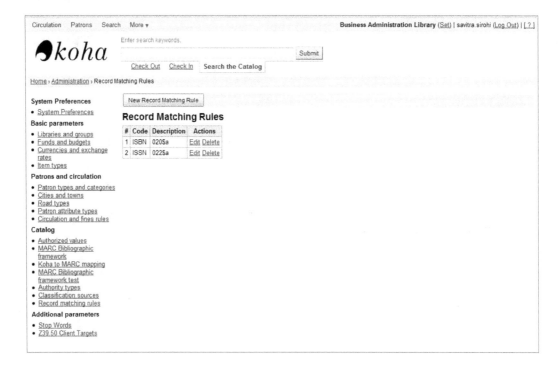

To create a new rule we use the **New Matching Rule** button.

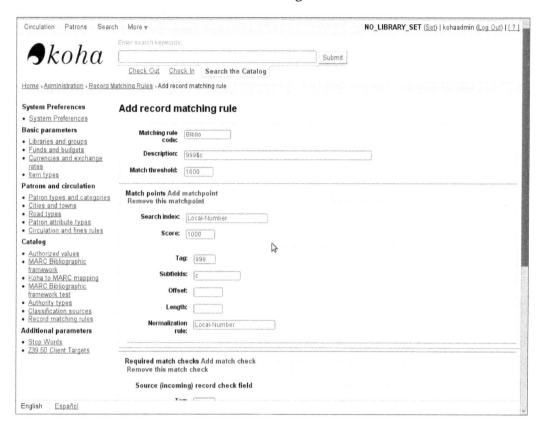

Understanding matching rules

Here are key points to note on creating matching rules:

- **Match points**: We will create one or more **match points**. Each match point refers to a catalog field that the incoming records in the import file and the existing records in the database are matched on. The match point could refer to fields such as Control number, Biblio number, or Title.

- **Match threshold**: Each matching rule has a threshold that must be crossed during the matching process for a record pair to be considered successfully matched.

- **Score**: Each match point in a matching rule is assigned a score. During the matching process if a pair of record is matched on the particular match point, the matched pair is assigned the corresponding score. The sum of scores across all match points must be greater than the **Match threshold**.

- **Match checks**: Optionally 1 or more match checks can be created for each matching rule. These checks compare a field in the incoming record to the same or different field in the records in the database. Think of these as an additional check to ensure records are correctly matched. For instance, if you have a **match point** on Title, you might want a match check based on author.

- **Search index**: This is the Zebra index that is used to match the records. See section *Determining search indexes* below for more information.

- **Tag and Subfield**: These refer to the MARC tag that the match point is based on.

- **Offset**: This refers to the number of characters of the match string that should be ignored when matching, the offset applies from the left of the string.

- **Length**: This refers to the number of characters of the match string that should be considered for matching. Using Offset and Length, we can match records based on certain parts of the values in MARC fields or subfields.

- **Normalization Rule**: This field is not used in the processing, and it does not matter what is entered here. Additional capabilities using different normalization rules may be added in newer versions of Koha.

Determining search indexes

We determine the search index by looking at two Zebra's configuration files — `ccl.properties` and `records.abs`. If an index is present in both files, it can be used in matching rules.

Let us say we wanted to update our bibliographic records after a cleanup, we could create a matching rule based on Koha's `biblionumber` database field. This is a unique number assigned to each bibliographic record and is stored in tag 999$c in the MARC record.

Let us take a look at Zebra's `record.abs` file in the folder `/etc/koha-dev/etc/zebradb/marc_defs/marc21/biblios/`:

```
linux-4yut:/usr/share/kohaclone/misc/migration_tools # vi /etc/koha-dev/
etc/zebradb/marc_defs/marc21/biblios/record.abs
```

If we run a search on tag 999$c, we find that the search index for this tag is `Local-Number`:

```
# Koha Local-Use Biblio Indexes
melm 999$c      Local-Number:n,Local-Number:w,Local-Number:s
```

Next we look at the file `ccl.properties` stored in the folder `/etc/koha-dev/etc/zebradb/`:

```
linux-4yut:/usr/share/kohaclone/misc/migration_tools # vi /etc/koha-dev/
etc/zebradb/ccl.properties
```

If we run a search on the index `Local-number`, we find an entry as follows:

```
Local-number 1=12
sn Local-number
```

The index `Local-number` is present in both these files and we can use it in the **Search index** field in matching rules.

More information and examples

For more information and examples on matching rules, refer to Koha community documentation on this topic, available at:

```
http://koha-community.org/documentation/3-2-manual/x3735#AEN4124.
```

Using LDAP with Koha

If your organization uses an LDAP (Lightweight Directory Access Protocol) server for user authentication, it makes sense to configure Koha to integrate with it. This way you don't have to maintain users and passwords in two places, the LDAP server and in Koha.

This is how Koha works with LDAP:

- When a user logs into Koha, the password entered by the user is verified against the password maintained on the LDAP server.

- We can configure Koha such that when a user logs in for the first time, his/her patron category, branch, address, and other such information is copied over into Koha.

- We can configure Koha such that if a user's LDAP record is updated, the updated information is copied over into Koha when the user next logs into Koha.

- We can map fields in the LDAP database to fields in Koha. This way we can make sure LDAP data is copied into Koha correctly.

It is fairly simple to configure Koha to use LDAP; let us take a look at a general example followed by the specific case of configuration for Microsoft Active Directory.

Configuring LDAP

To configure Koha to use LDAP, we edit the `/etc/koha-dev/etc/koha-conf.xml` file and add an LDAP block similar to this:

```
<useldapserver>1</useldapserver><!-- see C4::Auth_with_ldap for extra
configs you must add if you want to turn this on -->
<ldapserver id="ldapserver" listenref="ldapserver">
        <hostname>your hosts ip address or name</hostname>
        <base>base dn</base>
        <user>LDAP user's dn</user>
        <pass>LDAP user's password</pass>
        <replicate>1</replicate>        <!-- add new users from LDAP to
Koha database -->
        <update>1</update>             <!-- update existing users in Koha
database -->
        <auth_by_bind>1</auth_by_bind>
        <mapping>              <!-- match koha SQL field names to your
LDAP record field names -->
            <firstname   is="givenName"     ></firstname>
            <surname     is="sn"            ></surname>
            <userid is="uid"></userid>
            <password is="userPassword"   ></password>
            <email   is="mail"></email>
            <address is="address">Default Address</address>
            <city is="city">Default City</city>
            <branchcode is="branch">Default Branch Code</branchcode>
            <categorycode is="category">Default Catefory Code</
categorycode>
        </mapping>
    </ldapserver>
```

Here is how we configure the LDAP block:

1. Add the LDAP server block before these tags: `</config></yazgfs>` in the `koha-conf.xml` file.
2. Set the `<useldapserver>` tag to 1 to turn LDAP authentication on, set it to 0 to turn it off.
3. Enter the LDAP server's host name or IP address in the tag `<hostname>`.
4. Enter the LDAP server's base DN in the tag `<base>`.
5. In the tag `<user>` enter the DN of an LDAP user with browse privileges to the base DN.
6. Enter the LDAP user's password in the tag `<pass>`.
7. Set `<replicate>` tag to 1 if you want to create new users in Koha from the LDAP server. If this is set to 0, the user record must exist in Koha.

8. Set `<update>` tag to 1 if you want updates to user records on the LDAP server to update user records in Koha as well.

9. The fields listed in the `<mapping>` block refer to fields in the borrowers tables in Koha.

10. The fields listed in the `<mapping>` block must include all mandatory fields in the borrowers table except the field `borrowernumber`. Mandatory fields in the table are — surname, address, city, branchcode, and categorycode (patron category code).

11. The fields listed in the `<mapping>` block should include other Koha fields that have data in corresponding fields in the LDAP record. This way you can get useful data such as e-mail address or phone number from the LDAP record into Koha.

12. The name following `is=` refers to the corresponding field in the LDAP server.

13. For each field you can specify a default value in case the LDAP server does not have any value for that field.

Microsoft Active Directory

If you need to integrate Koha with Microsoft Active Directory, you may need to change the following in the LDAP block in the file `/etc/koha-dev/etc/koha-conf.xml` to get things to work:

- Set tag `<auth_by_bind>` to 1, like this:

```
<auth_by_bind>1</auth_by_bind> <!-- set to 1 to authenticate
by binding instead of password comparison, e.g., to use Active
Directory -->
```

- Set the `is` attribute for `userid` to `sAMAccountName` instead of UID. `sAMAccountName` is the corresponding uid field in Active Directory.

```
<userid       is="sAMAccountName" ></userid>
```

Setting permissions

If you use LDAP, you must set permissions for each individual staff user in Koha. To set permissions use the **Set Permissions** option under the **More** menu available in the details page for a patron.

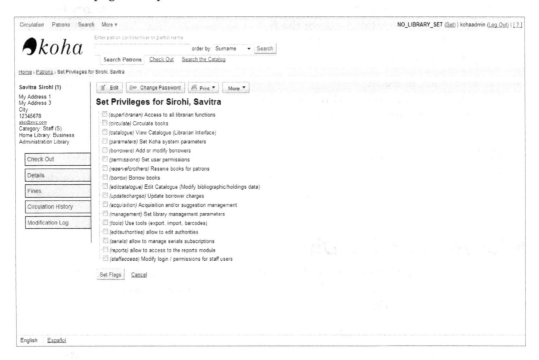

Multiple OPAC interfaces

If you have multiple libraries or branches on the same Koha installation, you might want to use the multiple OPAC interfaces feature of Koha.

We use this feature to:

- Create a customized OPAC interface for each library
- Each OPAC interface can have its own logo, colors, fonts, and so on.
- Search is limited to the particular library

Here are the steps to doing this:

1. Edit the Apache2 `koha-httpd.conf` file and create a virtual host block for each library or branch.

2. You will need domain names for each branch, for example, `branch1.mykohalibrary.org`, `branch2.mykohalibrary.org`.

3. In each virtual host, repeat this stanza, change the values of environment variables `OPAC_CSS_OVERRIDE` and `OPAC_SEARCH_LIMIT` appropriately.

```
SetEnv OPAC_CSS_OVERRIDE branch1.css
SetEnv OPAC_SEARCH_LIMIT branch:branch1
SetEnv OPAC_LIMIT_OVERRIDE 1
```

4. Create the corresponding style sheet files in the folder:

```
/koha-tmpl/opac-tmpl/prog/en/css/branch1.css
```

If we had two branches, we would have two Apache2 virtual hosts as follows:

```
## OPAC Virtual Host for Branch1
<VirtualHost *:80>
   ServerAdmin  webmaster@linux-4yut
   DocumentRoot /usr/share/kohaclone/koha-tmpl

   ServerName branch1.mykohalibrary.org
...

...


#  Repeat this virtualhost stanza changing the following environment vars
to
#  create multiple OPAC interfaces with custom css and/or search limits:
  SetEnv OPAC_CSS_OVERRIDE branch1.css
  SetEnv OPAC_SEARCH_LIMIT branch:branch1
  SetEnv OPAC_LIMIT_OVERRIDE 1

</VirtualHost>


## OPAC Virtual Host for Branch2
<VirtualHost *:80>
   ServerAdmin  webmaster@linux-4yut
   DocumentRoot /usr/share/kohaclone/koha-tmpl

   ServerName branch2.mykohalibrary.org
...

...


#  Repeat this virtualhost stanza changing the following environment vars
to
#  create multiple OPAC interfaces with custom css and/or search limits:
  SetEnv OPAC_CSS_OVERRIDE branch2.css
  SetEnv OPAC_SEARCH_LIMIT branch:branch2
  SetEnv OPAC_LIMIT_OVERRIDE 1

</VirtualHost>
```

Installing new languages

If you need to have Koha OPAC and staff client screens in another language, you will need to install the particular language. Here are the steps involved:

1. Install Perl module prerequisite `Locale::PO`.
2. Check availability of the corresponding language files in the Koha folder.
3. Create new folders for the new language in the appropriate OPAC and staff client folders.
4. Use Koha's program—`tmpl_process2.pl` to install the new language.
5. Enable the new language via Koha's system preferences module.

As an example let us install the Spanish language.

Install Locale::PO module

We need the Perl module `Locale::PO` before we can install the new language. We use CPAN to install this module:

```
koha@li190-245:~/kohaclone$ cpan Locale::PO
```

Creating language templates for the OPAC

First let us locate the Spanish language files in the `kohaclone` folder. The language files have an extension `.po` and are found in the `misc/translator` folder:

```
koha@li190-245:~/kohaclone $ cd misc/translator/
koha@li190-245:~/kohaclone/misc/translator $ ls *ES*.po

es-ES-i-opac-t-prog-v-3000000.po

es-ES-i-staff-t-prog-v-3000000.po
```

To create the language templates for the OPAC, first we create a new directory for the new language in the `koha-tmpl/opac-tmpl/prog/` folder:

```
koha@li190-245:~/kohaclone/misc/translator # mkdir ../../koha-tmpl/opac-tmpl/prog/es
```

We then use the `tmpl_process3.pl` program to install the new language. The program is executed as follows:

```
koha@li190-245:~/kohaclone/misc/translator # perl tmpl_process3.pl
install -i <path to the English language folder> -o <path to the new
language folder> -s <path to the .po file of the new language> -r
```

We would install the Spanish language file for the OPAC in this fashion:

```
koha@li190-245:~/kohaclone/misc/translator # perl tmpl_process3.pl
install -i ../../koha-tmpl/opac-tmpl/prog/en/ -o ../../koha-tmpl/opac-
tmpl/prog/es/ -s po/es-ES-i-opac-t-prog-v-3000000.po -r
```

Creating language templates for the staff client

In a similar fashion, we can create the language templates for the staff client. First we create the folder for Spanish language, this time in the /koha-tmpl/intranet-tmpl/prog/ folder:

```
linux-4yut:/usr/share/kohaclone/misc/translator # mkdir ../../koha-tmpl/
intranet-tmpl/prog/es
```

And then we use the tmpl_process3.pl program to install the new language:

```
linux-4yut:/usr/share/kohaclone/misc/translator # perl tmpl_process3.
pl install -i ../../koha-tmpl/intranet-tmpl/prog/en/ -o ../../koha-tmpl/
intranet-tmpl/prog/es/ -s po/es-ES-i-staff-t-prog-v-3000000.po -r
```

System preferences

Once the language is installed, don't forget to enable these from the **I18N/L10N** (short form of Internationalization and Localization) block in the **Global System Preferences** section under **Koha Administration**.

Here are the system preferences you will need to change:

- **language**: Use this preference to enable the new language for the staff client
- **opaclanguages**: Use this preference to enable the new language for the OPAC
- **opaclangaugesdisplay**: Choose whether you want to display a language selection bar on the OPAC

Testing the new language

Once the system preferences are set correctly, you should see the new language in the language selection bar at the bottom of the page in the OPAC and the staff client.

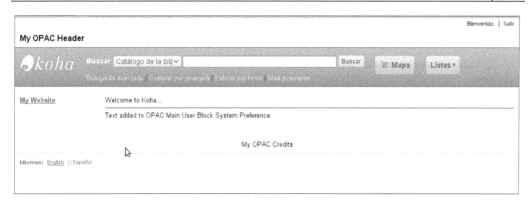

Setting up a public Z39.50 server

With Koha you can publish your catalog records to the outside world via the Z39.50 protocol. This will allow any Z39.50 compliant client software to search and copy records from your catalog. Some applications of this feature are:

- Allow other libraries to copy records from your catalog
- Include your catalog data in results of a Z39.50 compliant federated search tool in use in your organization

Configuring your Koha to be a Z39.50 server is not that hard; we cover the steps below.

We edit the `koha-conf.xml` file to configure the public Z39.50 server:

```
koha@li190-245:~/kohaclone$ vi /etc/koha-dev/etc/koha-conf.xml
```

Configuring the listen directive

The listen directive controls the network protocol, the IP address and the port that our public server will be available on.

To set up the listen directive for the public server, remove the comment tags on the listen directive for the public server:

```
<!-- public server runs on tcp -->
 <listen id="publicserver" >tcp:@:9999</listen>
```

The @ symbol signifies all IP addresses, so the public Z39.50 server will listen on any and all IP addresses on the machine. You can set up a specific IP address here if you like, something like:

```
<!-- public server runs on tcp -->
 <listen id="publicserver" >tcp:192.168.1.123:9999</listen>
```

The `9999` after the colon in the lines above is the port the server will listen on. You can change this as well, to something like this:

```
<!-- public server runs on tcp -->
 <listen id="publicserver" >tcp:192.168.1.123:7090</listen>
```

Configuring the server directive

Next we add a `server` directive. This directive essentially sets up a new Zebra server. As part of this directive we configure things such as the location of Zebra indexes folders, location of Zebra's bibliographic configuration files, the MARC record syntax to be used, or the location of the style sheets to be used for transforming the records.

The simplest thing to do is to model our new server on the existing bibliographic server block already configured in the `koha-conf.xml` file:

```
<server id="biblioserver"  listenref="biblioserver">
    <directory>/etc/koha-dev/var/lib/zebradb/biblios</directory>
    <config>/etc/koha-dev/etc/zebradb/zebra-biblios.cfg</config>
    <cql2rpn>/etc/koha-dev/etc/zebradb/pqf.properties</cql2rpn>
```

Once we copy this block, we replace the name `biblioserver` with `publicserver`, like so:

```
<server id="publicserver"  listenref="publicserver">
    <directory>/etc/koha-dev/var/lib/zebradb/biblios</directory>
    <config>/etc/koha-dev/etc/zebradb/zebra-biblios.cfg</config>
    <cql2rpn>/etc/koha-dev/etc/zebradb/pqf.properties</cql2rpn>
```

Configuring the serverinfo directive

And finally we configure the `serverinfo` directive. This directive controls the location to a Zebra configuration file and the username and password that allows access to the Zebra indexes.

Again, it is best to model the new `serverinfo` directive on the corresponding directive for the bibliographic server:

```
<serverinfo id="biblioserver">
        <ccl2rpn>/etc/koha-dev/etc/zebradb/ccl.properties</ccl2rpn>
        <user>kohauser</user>
        <password>zebrastripes</password>
</serverinfo>
```

We just copy this block above and replace the ID `biblioserver` with `publicserver`, like so:

```
<serverinfo id="publicserver">
        <ccl2rpn>/etc/koha-dev/etc/zebradb/ccl.properties</ccl2rpn>
        <user>kohauser</user>
        <password>zebrastripes</password>
</serverinfo>
```

Restarting the Zebra server

To make sure the Zebra server uses the updated configurations we have just performed, we restart `zebrasrv`:

```
linux-4yut:/home/koha # sudo /etc/init.d/koha-zebra-daemon restart
```

Summary

In this final chapter we looked at some advanced features of Koha:

- The ability to create one's own record matching rules gives us a powerful way to import new records and to update and maintain the catalog.

- Many large organization use LDAP to maintain users and passwords. Koha can talk to any LDAP server including Microsoft Active Directory. The configuration is simple; however, attention must be paid to the replicate, update, and the mapping fields.

- To setup customized OPACs for each library or branch that share a Koha system, we set up separate Apache2 virtual hosts for each branch. For each virtual host we set up the corresponding domain name, the name of the stylesheet file, and the branch code.

- To install additional languages, we learned how to use the `tmpl_process3. pl` program to install language files.

- Setting up a Z39.50 server allows us to share our catalog with others and to include it in other Z39.50 solutions such as federated search.

Index

H

holds preferences
  configuring 107
  editing 107

I

idmap, Bulkmarcimport.pl option 174
imports tools, Koha
  about 171
  bulkmarckimport.pl 172
  GUI import tool 175
  MARCEdit 172
installation
  Zebra 41
installation packages, Koha installation
  Debian/Ubuntu package lists 14
  Perl modules 13, 14
  system packages 13
installation tools, Koha
  CPAN shell 9
  Git 9
  make utility 9
  package manager 9
IP based virtual hosts 24
Item types
  about 94
  creating 96
  identifying 95

K

Koha
  Apache2, auto-starting 61
  cataloging configuration tools 68
  cataloging module 67
  circulation module 91
  community resources 196
  crontab, configuring 58
  features 245
  general preferences, configuring 138
  global system preferences module 112
  heads 218
  installing, with Zebra 42
  matching rules 247
  matching rules for use during catalog
    imports, creating 246, 247

matching rules for use during catalog
    imports, using 246, 247
  multiple OPAC interfaces 252, 253
  MySQL, auto-starting 61
  new languages, installing 254
  OPAC preferences, configuring 122
  search indexes, determining 248, 249
  software branches 218
  software stack installation 16
  styling and appearance, configuring 132
  system preferences 111
  tags 218
  transactional modules, configuring 113
  using, without Zebra 48, 49
  version, selecting 219
  web installer, executing 51
  working with LDAP 249
  XML SAX parser, configuring 62
  Zebra related components 40
  Zebra server, auto-starting 61
Koha 3.0 user manual
  URL 113
Koha 3.2 manual
  URL 113
Koha administrative fields
  branch codes, setting up 179
  collection codes, setting up 181
  item types, setting up 180
  shelving locations, setting up 182
Koha application folder structure
  about 228
  relationships, between files 229
  template files 229
  top level folders 228
Koha architecture 8
Koha bug tracker 197
kohaclone folder
  c4 228
  etc 228
  installer 228
  koha-tmpl 228
  Perl scripts 228
Koha community documentation
  URL 249
KOHA_CONF environment variable
  setting up 63

Thank you for buying
Koha 3 Library Management System

About Packt Publishing

Packt, pronounced 'packed', published its first book *"Mastering phpMyAdmin for Effective MySQL Management"* in April 2004 and subsequently continued to specialize in publishing highly focused books on specific technologies and solutions.

Our books and publications share the experiences of your fellow IT professionals in adapting and customizing today's systems, applications, and frameworks. Our solution based books give you the knowledge and power to customize the software and technologies you're using to get the job done. Packt books are more specific and less general than the IT books you have seen in the past. Our unique business model allows us to bring you more focused information, giving you more of what you need to know, and less of what you don't.

Packt is a modern, yet unique publishing company, which focuses on producing quality, cutting-edge books for communities of developers, administrators, and newbies alike. For more information, please visit our website: www.packtpub.com.

About Packt Open Source

In 2010, Packt launched two new brands, Packt Open Source and Packt Enterprise, in order to continue its focus on specialization. This book is part of the Packt Open Source brand, home to books published on software built around Open Source licences, and offering information to anybody from advanced developers to budding web designers. The Open Source brand also runs Packt's Open Source Royalty Scheme, by which Packt gives a royalty to each Open Source project about whose software a book is sold.

Writing for Packt

We welcome all inquiries from people who are interested in authoring. Book proposals should be sent to author@packtpub.com. If your book idea is still at an early stage and you would like to discuss it first before writing a formal book proposal, contact us; one of our commissioning editors will get in touch with you.

We're not just looking for published authors; if you have strong technical skills but no writing experience, our experienced editors can help you develop a writing career, or simply get some additional reward for your expertise.

Linux Email

ISBN: 978-1-847198-64-8   Paperback: 376 pages

Set up, maintain, and secure a small office email server

1. Covers all the information you need to easily set up your own Linux email server

2. Learn how to provide web access to email, virus and spam protection, and more

3. Thoroughly covers open source tools like PostFix, Courier, SpamAssassin, and ProcMail

4. A step-by-step approach where the reader is taken through examples with ample screenshots and clear explanations to facilitate learning

Linux Thin Client Networks Design and Deployment

ISBN: 978-1-847192-04-2   Paperback: 176 pages

A quick guide for System Administrators

1. Learn to implement the right Linux thin client network for your requirements

2. Evaluate and choose the right hardware and software for your deployment

3. Techniques to intelligently design and set up your thin client network

4. Practical advice on educating users, convincing management, and intelligent use of legacy systems

Please check **www.PacktPub.com** for information on our titles

www.ingramcontent.com/pod-product-compliance
Lightning Source LLC
Chambersburg PA
CBHW060522060326
40690CB00017B/3355